Tea at the Blue Lantern Inn

Tea at the Blue Lantern Inn

A SOCIAL HISTORY OF
THE TEA ROOM CRAZE IN AMERICA

JAN WHITAKER

ST. MARTIN'S PRESS ❧ NEW YORK

Book Design by Gretchen Achilles

www.stmartins.com

Library of Congress Cataloging-in-Publication Data

Whitaker, Jan

    Tea at the Blue Lantern Inn: a social history of the tea room craze in America / Jan Whitaker.—1st ed.

       p.cm

    Includes bibliographical references and index.

    ISBN 0-312-29064-0

       1. Tearooms—United States—History. 2. United States—Social life and customs. I. Title

TX945.W44 2002

647.9573—dc21

2002069651

FIRST EDITION: DECEMBER 2002

10 9 8 7 6 5 4 3 2 1

In memory of my mother,

Gean O'Hara Britt,

who loved to eat in tea rooms

CONTENTS

ACKNOWLEDGMENTS

The author who picks an unexplored topic such as the history of tea rooms is going to need a lot of help. I combed through thousands of books, dusty files, and moldering magazines, aided by dozens of helpful guides. In response to my requests, many librarians descended into nether regions to retrieve old periodicals that rarely see the light of day. Libraries and archives deserving special mention are: the Chicago Historical Society; the William L. Clements Library, University of Michigan; the John Crerar Library, University of Chicago; Forbes Library, Northampton, Massachusetts; the Historical Association of Southern Florida; the Library of Congress; the New York Public Library; the Smith

College Archives; the Schlesinger Library, Radcliffe Institute; the National Museum of American History, the Smithsonian Institution; and, above all, the W. E. B. Du Bois Library, University of Massachusetts, Amherst.

I gathered my collection of vintage tea room postcards aided by the eagle eyes and wide acquisition powers of several leading antiquarian paper sellers. Prominent among them were postcard dealers Joe Battista, Don and Newly Preziosi, Jose Rodriguez, and Ove Braskerud. Scholarly book dealer Kenneth Schoen delivered an important and hard-to-find book. Thanks also to the many sellers on e-Bay who together provide a treasure trove of historic images and documents.

Many authors, scholars, and collectors provided information, inspiration, and support. Warren Belasco's discussion of tea rooms in his history of early twentieth-century motor trips, *Americans on the Road*, whetted my appetite to know more and launched my project, and Harvey Levenstein's remarkable books on the history of food and dining carried me further. Both authors kindly answered my questions, as did John Egerton, an expert on Southern food. Melanie Solomon shared with me her master's thesis on tea rooms in New York State. Jane and Michael Stern, whose lively and witty writing has brought recognition to local eating places in America, were helpful beyond my expectation. Kathleen Bergstrom shared her wonderful collection of vintage tea room menus, as well as her own knowledge and appreciation of tea rooms.

Professional help and moral support were forthcoming from many sources. I am thankful to Pat Kelly of the Culinary Historians of Boston; to the National Writers Union, especially members Miryam Williamson, Marietta Pritchard, Steve Simurda, B.J. Roche, and Bruce Carson; to Lynne Layton and Ellen Pader, good friends who gave enthusiastic encouragement; to my energetic and upbeat literary agent, Linda Roghaar; and to my excellent editor at St. Martin's, Marian Lizzi, to copy editor Steve Boldt, and to all the fine designers, publicists, and associates at the press.

Barton Byg, my life partner, was helpful in every way mentioned above and then some. Had I decided to go to the North Pole for research, within minutes he would have been on the phone making our travel arrangements. I couldn't have done it without him, and probably wouldn't even have wanted to.

Tea at the Blue Lantern Inn

Welcome to the Tea Room

The twentieth century witnessed profound changes in women's role in American society. At the beginning of the century American women were dressed in long, restrictive clothing and had no vote. They could not travel freely nor go many places alone. By century's end, women held public office across the land and ventured anywhere, even beyond the earth's atmosphere. The tea room did not cause all these changes, but it did play a role in bringing women out into society and into the business world. In doing so, it left a mark and changed many restaurant customs in ways little appreciated today. One hundred or so years later, our cultural memory of the tea room is mummified into a slightly ridiculous stereotype, identified with little old ladies, white gloves, and extreme propriety. We have forgotten its vivacity, modernity, stylishness—and playful silliness—and have lost our ability to imagine many of those little old ladies in the free-spirited orange-and-black tea rooms of their youth.

Transportation, Temperance, and Women

The story of the creation of the American tea room is intertwined with three other early-twentieth-century stories: the advent of the automobile, the movement to prohibit alcohol, and women's ongoing quest for independence. The growing use of automobiles is especially important in the development of one early quintessential type of tea room, that located along the roadside in rural areas outside cities.

Put a woman in a car—often in the driver's seat—ban alcohol from public establishments, and voilà! Dotted across the American landscape of cities and towns of the teens and twenties spring up little eating places serving light lunches, simple suppers, and dainty afternoon teas to her and her friends rambling about in small automobile touring parties.

THE
SKIPPER
HE SERVES
THE THINGS
YOU LIKE
AT
15 Liberty St.
Nantucket

Picture a woman in South Sudbury, Massachusetts, putting down her spoon and bowl and taking off her apron as she hears an approaching car. She opens the front door of her Cape Cod cottage and greets her guests, a group of four youngish Bostonians out for a Sunday spin. After driving exactly twenty-two miles from Boston's Copley Square on this July day, they are not only hungry, but hot and thirsty too. They sit down at one of the small tables in her converted living room, scanning the room for antiques and hooked rugs (as they always do when they're in the country). They don't know it, but the proprietor has filled the room with items she's selling on commission—and

Nobscot
Mt.
Tea
House
At the Sign of the Black Tea Kettle

she's hoping they'll ask if anything's for sale. They then consult the neatly hand-lettered little menu. Creamed Chicken on Toast. Nut and Jelly Sandwich. Pear and Ginger Salad. Iced Tea (or Iced Coffee), Lemonade, and Grape Juice. A simple scene, yet one that captured the imagination of American women as few could. In magazine after magazine, stories about tea rooms like this one created an immense wave of interest in readers who longed to run "a tea room of their very own."

The group of Bostonians that Sunday in the summer of 1923 were among a rather select handful of Americans who owned or operated automobiles. In 1920, 8 million passenger cars were registered in this country, compared to the 200 million on the roads today. Cars were regarded primarily as recreational vehicles, rather than dependable means of transportation. Most Americans relied on trains, trolleys, and their own two feet to get where they were going. Cars broke down or had to have tires replaced with almost predictable regularity; the roads were terrible, many unpaved and deeply rutted. Our foursome from Boston, however, were luckier than most. Living in the densely populated East, they had more paved roads to drive on. Their route from Boston was detailed in a thick green guide book that told them where to turn and where they could find a garage if they had car trouble. It was "practically all tarred macadam or concrete," the book said, and was marked with red signs on poles along the way. Paved roads meant more cars on the move, and as a consequence

more business for country tea rooms. The greater number of paved roads in New England is probably why there were more roadside tea rooms there than anywhere else in the country.

We might also assume the Boston group disapproved of people who drank. Even before it was banned outright nationwide in 1920, alcohol consumption was viewed with disfavor by the teetotaling middle class who patronized tea rooms (some of which borrowed the abbreviated T from the temperance campaign, calling themselves T-houses). Prohibition closed many of the nation's finest hotels and restaurants, dependent as they were upon income from spirits to subsidize the French cuisine served in their dining rooms. Surprisingly, many people of comfortable means who could afford to eat in the best places didn't seem to care much. If shutting down the liquor industry eliminated the saloons and took drunks off the street, upstanding middle-class citizens were more than willing to forgo the occasional lavish dinner at Delmonico's or Sherry's in New York (or their Kansas City or Cleveland equivalents). In fact, many seemed to prefer simple sandwich shops, tea rooms, and even the newfangled cafeterias for their meals. Young people liked the informality of tea rooms and lunch counters, where customers could dress as they liked, nibble on a toasted sandwich instead of a five-course dinner, and just "hang out."

Prohibition truly leveled the playing field for would-be restaurateurs. The absence of the liquor industry on the restaurant scene made it much easier for newcomers, often women, to find a niche in what had once been an intimidating business. Being a restaurateur in the "wet" days involved stocking expensive wine cellars, dealing with alcohol purveyors, and catering to the dining, drinking, and cigar-smoking requirements of a predominantly male, and often rowdy, clientele. Furthermore the restaurant business was closely associated in many people's minds with catering to appetites of all kinds, including sexual appetites. For a woman to enter this business at the turn of the century, even as an unescorted patron, was a risk to her reputation.

This takes us to the motives of our women protagonists. This is a more complicated saga about the need to make a living, the wish to be independent and get out in public, the dream of having a business of one's own, and the longing to stray away from the mainstream and have a more adventurous life. It's about women as business owners, operators, managers, hostesses, cooks, and—very important—as customers. Of course, tea rooms, tea houses, tea shops, and tea gardens, as they were variously called, were sometimes operated and patronized by men too, but they were mostly women's projects, run with a woman's touch and greatly loved by their faithful women customers.

At the heart of the story of women who ran the tea rooms is their need to find a public expression for their creativity. During the 1920s, at the height of the tea room craze, these little businesses were virtually synonymous with female self-expression. It seemed there were almost no women in America who didn't harbor a wish to run a tea room, decorate it (very important), and supervise every small detail. How many tea room patrons imagined they were doing market research as they tried out all the new places in town, making mental notes of how they would do things differently, better?

Even the hostile reaction of men in the business world confirmed that women's enthusiasm for tea rooms was a new force to be reckoned with. Wise-guy commentary of the times said that most tea rooms should be named My Wife's

POLLY'S PATIO
TEA SHOP
3033 West Seventh at Shatto Place
LOS ANGELES

Tea Room because husbands were footing the bill for these expensive, money-losing projects. Whatever grain of truth was behind this observation, it was no doubt bolstered by a generous dose of disapproval aimed at women entering the business world. Banks were reluctant to loan money, and suppliers were none too ready to open accounts for fledgling tea room operators. "Start small" was the advice given by correspondence courses and business consultants. Usually there was no choice. Those who began businesses did so on a shoestring, or with their own small hoard of capital.

It's true that many tea room owners were inexperienced amateurs, with little knowledge of how to run a business, much less a tough restaurant business. Others, however, had learned the ropes working for the Schrafft's chain or other restaurants and knew what it took to keep a food business afloat. Still others were graduates of cooking schools or domestic science departments at big universities such as Iowa and Cornell. Many were schoolteachers who had teamed up with a friend during the summer to run a tea room in a vacation spot. There were mother-and-daughter teams, sister teams, and husband-and-wife teams, along with many who went it alone. Among all the failures—and there were plenty—were many success stories of thriving businesses built up from the flimsiest of beginnings.

Tea room development was almost certainly linked to feminists' plans around the turn of the twentieth century to substitute communal kitchens for meal preparation in the home. Direct links are hard to find, but tea room consultant Ralph Noyes Elliott wrote in 1926 that the tea room, as it had developed as a type of small restaurant by the 1920s, was an outgrowth of "a plan to promote the communistic preparation of food," a plan that failed but whose "governing and underlying principle" was applied by "increasingly independent women" to tea rooms. Evolving from "a hermetically sealed lodge of some secret society of women," he said, the tea room had come to resemble a home dining room serving simple yet well-prepared meals to men, women, and children.

A few connections between tea rooms and communal dining schemes can be sketched. The books of Charlotte Perkins Gilman, which conceptualized feminist apartment buildings and kitchenless homes, were popular among women in the early home economics movement. Home economists were well represented among the ranks of tea room owners and managers. Also, Henrietta Rodman, who was behind the plans for the Liberal Club's restaurant in Greenwich Village, an inspiration for many of the area's tea rooms, raised money in 1914 to create Gilman's apartment house in the Village. Although designs were completed for the twelve-story building, which was to have child-care facilities, maid service, and all meals provided in dining rooms, it was never built. But clearly Rodman's plans as well as the idea that restaurants were public services that freed women from cooking duties in the home were well known in Greenwich Village, and beyond.

Mah-Jongg, College Girls, and Candy Stores

Also intertwined with the flowering of tea rooms was the growth of that major something-for-everybody institution found in the center of every American city, the department store. And the story of the tea room is also tied up with the woes of the independent candy store, the "eating-out habit" of city people, a desire to connect eating to entertainment, and a tendency toward lighter food in the American diet. It corresponded to the rise of a middle class with spending money, the expansion of the suburbs, the popularity of bridge and mah-jongg parties, more women getting college educations, and the influence of home economics and the Colonial Revival movement. The development of tea rooms was even linked to reverence for the father of our country, George Washington. Back in the nineteenth century, women had acquired the tea-drinking habit as they held Martha Washington teas to raise funds for churches and other causes and to commemorate the first president and the first first lady.

Tea Rooms by Other Names

To make matters confusing, tea rooms weren't always named as such, and conversely, some places that were called tea rooms more nearly resembled snack shops, or even nightclubs. After Prohibition ended, some tea rooms began to serve alcoholic beverages, while retaining the appellation *tea room*. Also, along with tea rooms, there were tea houses, tea shops, and tea gardens, as well as a fair number of coffee and chocolate shops that served afternoon tea and in most respects were identical to tea rooms. The name *tea room* itself implied a room or rooms in a larger business, such as a store or hotel, but was often also used generically to describe a stand-alone business. *Tea house* typically referred to a tea business run in a detached house, while *tea shop* typically pertained to a storefront business. During the 1920s the term *shop* became fashionable, and businesses selling everything from dresses to candy to tea adopted this name to sound exclusive. Seasonal businesses with tables outdoors, particularly in resort areas, often called themselves tea gardens.

A DINING PLACE WITH OLD WORLD CHARM

Prince Murat Coffee House
250 ST. GEORGE STREET

Breakfast
Luncheon
Afternoon Tea
Dinner

Cakes, Pies
Motor and
Picnic Lunches
To Order

FRANCES R. IRVINE   PHONE 382   ST. AUGUSTINE, FLA.

Contrary to what their name suggests, tea rooms didn't necessarily revolve around tea, the beverage, nor tea, the repast. In the beginning, around the turn of the twentieth century, some tea rooms did serve only one "meal," afternoon tea, which did indeed feature the beverage tea. This situation would not last long, however, for a variety of financial reasons. Even if they were high priced (which they were), these establishments could not make enough money on afternoon teas alone, and future growth seemed limited since Americans simply weren't all that devoted to drinking tea or taking an afternoon break. British visitors criticized the inferior grades of tea served in America and were horrified at how improperly the leaves were brewed. Restaurant trade journals stressed that water had to be at full boil to make tea correctly, a basic concept that evidently was by no means universally grasped. Coffee was as popular as tea, even in tea rooms, and lunch service was more lucrative than afternoon tea.

THE SIGN OF THE 601

𝕭𝖔𝖞𝖑𝖘𝖙𝖔𝖓 𝕾𝖙𝖗𝖊𝖊𝖙 𝕭𝖔𝖘𝖙𝖔𝖓

Indeed, American tea rooms were in fact small restaurants, serving mainly lunch and, secondarily, dinner. What is especially significant about them is that they introduced new ways of doing things to an all-male restaurant industry. They were novel because they marked the entry of American operators into what had been a largely European-influenced industry. They demonstrated that women were now a class of customers who had money to spend, who made their own decisions, and whose preferences were both highly defined and often quite different from men's. The restaurant industry, reeling from Prohibition and a shifting customer base, couldn't help but become curious about these annoying new ventures. Like Sigmund Freud, industry experts asked themselves for the first time: What do women want? The answers were sometimes surprising and not always what the etiquette books prescribed.

Tea rooms developed a cuisine all their own. Their food was a freewheeling blend of simplified French and New England plain, with a preference for fresh ingredients and simplicity in preparation. Tea room cooks apparently felt any recipe could be improved with the addition of liberal amounts of butter, cream, and mayonnaise. The sandwich, the salad, and the casserole came into their own on tea room menus, and home-style desserts were perfected and made elegant. Tea room operators staked their reputations on home-cooking standards, while denouncing everyday restaurant trickery. They promised to remain true to the standards of middle-class mothers who would never consciously serve spoiled or substandard food to their families. Tea room cuisine had its highs and its lows, its marshmallows and its handmade mayonnaise. It blended the chic and the corny, old traditions and new twists.

1890s to 1950s

In a sense the story of tea rooms could begin and end with the department store, since their tea rooms spanned the period from the 1890s to the 1950s. In the mid-nineteenth century, the department store became the first institution to draw women in numbers into the previously all-male city center. The department store was a world unto itself, complete with children's playrooms and spacious women's lounges furnished with writing desks and easy chairs. With bureaus for paying bills and repairing watches, gloves, and shoes, and departments selling almost every retail item known, these wonders of commerce also contained eating places for their customers. As the custom of afternoon tea

The Copper Kettle Tea Room

223 MERCANTILE PLACE

THE FIRST TEA ROOM IN LOS ANGELES, CALIFORNIA

became more fashionable around the turn of the twentieth century, department stores restyled their rather drab dining rooms, added chandeliers and potted palms, and christened them tea rooms.

In this book the tea room story will begin with its high-fashion expression, the hotel tea room, and end with the department store tea room, the last survivor of the tea room era of the early twentieth century. The chapters are presented roughly in chronological order, although many of the different types of tea rooms actually overlapped in time. As noted earlier, the peak decade for tea rooms was the 1920s. Tea rooms were still around in the 1930s and 1940s, although the Depression and wartime took a toll on the business. After the war, apart from those in department stores, the tea room no longer thrived and was considered the old lady of the restaurant industry.

HIGH SOCIETY

The hotel tea room of the early twentieth century specialized in afternoon tea. Not needing to make a profit from this service, the best hotels went out of their way to cater to the urban elite whose favor they wished to win. Fur-clad, perfumed women in high-heeled shoes, often accompanied by male escorts, added to the cachet of the establishment as they crowded into the elaborate public tea rooms and salons often conspicuously situated in the lobbies of grand hotels. Other elite tea rooms, independently operated, also opened in big cities around 1900. The haute bourgeois associations of this era would stick to the Fifth Avenue and Main Street tea rooms for a long time, suggesting tea rooms were places catering only to the well-dressed and affluent.

VERMILLION HOUNDS AND GREEN WITCHES

For every trend there is a countertrend. City tea rooms would continue to be exclusively associated with high society only until Greenwich Villagers came along around 1915 and upset the tea cart, making fun of pretentiousness and mocking uptown tea rooms with irreverent takeoffs. Shock waves of delight spread throughout the nation. Would-be Greenwich Villages sprang up on crooked streets in towns across the country—all fitted out with smoky tea room haunts frequented by gender-role challenging "short-haired women and long-haired men." Even more significant, as Main Street soon realized, a new marketing technique had now been introduced onto the American eatery scene, one represented by playful names, artsy interiors, impromptu entertainment, and costumed waitpersons.

WAFFLES AND GIFTS

At the same time as Greenwich Village tea rooms were emerging, the rural New England–style tea room, which had begun around 1910, was chugging right along, increasingly specializing in chicken and waffle dinners, and adding gift shops, overnight accommodations, and gas pumps out front. Everything was designed to capture the tourist dollar, and yet these enterprises remained surprisingly uncommercial, just like their successors, the country inns and bed-and-breakfasts of today. Throughout the 1920s, 1930s, and 1940s, roadside tea shops and tea houses spread across much of the United States, even making it into the South, an area supplied with relatively few restaurants until after the Second World War.

FOREVER COLONIAL?

The New England type of tea room, along with Colonial Revival architecture of the 1920s, was responsible for popularizing Early American decor and themes in eating places, an effect that would last for decades. Their Colonial copper kettles, weather vanes, and homey hearths would eventually be appropriated by highway and shopping-mall chain restaurants of the 1960s, growing tiresome by the end of that decade. But during the teens and twenties, Colonial decor seemed like a refreshing break from the dark carpets, overstuffed furniture, and heavy draperies of the Victorian period. It became the epitome of "good taste," separating the best roadside and suburban tea rooms from downscale wannabes. Other versions of "historical" charm were also developed in early tea rooms, including Dutch, Mission, and just-plain-quaint styles.

CITIFIED

In the eating-out era of the 1920s, most restaurants were not located on the roadside, but in well-populated cities. This was true of tea rooms as well. The larger the city, the more tea rooms there were to choose from. With twenty-nine tea rooms on one block alone, West Forty-ninth Street in Manhattan may have had the honor of having the most of these establishments of any one street in the United States. A restaurant trade journal reported in 1925 that New York City had eight thousand tea rooms! Did a careless typesetter add an extra zero? In fact, no one knows just how many tea rooms there were across the country, but in the 1920s tea room chains developed, many connected to candy stores. Metropolitan tea rooms were not confined to city cores, spreading throughout the 1920s to the suburbs, where they attracted whole families.

TEA LEAVES AND SYMPATHY

During the Great Depression of the 1930s, tea room owners looked for new ways to attract patrons. Prohibition was lifted in this decade, with

beer coming back first and then hard liquor, putting pressure on tea rooms to hold on to and widen their clientele. Some tea rooms dissolved their identities as they opened cocktail lounges. But others introduced Gypsy themes and tea-leaf readings to appeal to less affluent young workingwomen. The tea room of this time was all about escape, just as were the thriving motion pictures of the 1930s, and tea rooms continued a trend begun in the 1920s, borrowing the techniques of stage-set designers to dramatically enhance their interiors.

SIXTH FLOOR!

Coming full circle, we wrap up with the department store. With Greenwich Village bohemian tea shops and Depression-era Gypsy tea rooms submerged in the past and all but forgotten, post-WWII Americans now saw the dowager department-store tea room as just the place to train their daughters in the pillbox-hatted and white-gloved ways of "traditional" ladylike behavior. The venerable tea-room-without-saying-so, Schrafft's, also assumed this role. In department stores across America in the 1950s, crustless chicken-salad sandwiches and petits fours were fastidiously consumed by twelve-year-old girls surrounded by mothers, aunts, and grandmothers, as all watched fashion shows mounted on specially erected runways.

✧ ✧ ✧

This book is intended to fill in some of the many blanks of tea room history, eradicate the idea that they were mainly for "old ladies in white gloves," celebrate their great variety, and add a colorful chapter to the history of American women's popular culture.

CHAPTER ONE

Society Sips

To-day, at the tea-hour smart carriages are drawn up in front of the tea-room;
within, the merry tap of high heels on polished floors mingles with the fresh odor
of violets and the rustle of many skirts. It is the fashion to drink tea in New York!

—HARPER'S BAZAR, MARCH 1908

The emergence of public places to drink afternoon tea and consume light refreshments around the turn of the century brought
out high society and advertised to the world that tea was a classy
affair, a connotation that would hover around the tea room for years to
come. Unlike the lunch counter, cafeteria, and coffee shop—all of which
were becoming popular as places to eat and drink—the tea room's
charms were not for everyone.

Afternoon tea was so fashionable with the leisure class that hotels began serving it in their lounges and lobbies, and even transforming their
dining rooms into tea rooms between four and six each afternoon. By

1910 hotel managers were noticing that their tea rooms were outdoing their barrooms in liveliness and good cheer and were adding substantial revenue. Hotels began to dedicate special rooms to the tea custom. In a few big cities a sprinkling of independent, usually small, tea rooms sprang up around the same time. Women's clubs too installed tea rooms. One of the most fashionable was New York City's Colony Club, which had a tea room decorated in 1907 by the famed Elsie de Wolfe, the first woman to become successful in the male-dominated decorator trade. Done in green, with trellises on the wall and a fountain in the corner, it established an iconic style for chic tea rooms before the First World War.

Tea drinking in America had long been associated with the elite. The beverage was imported and thus expensive, both before and after the Boston Tea Party. The tea-drinking custom was also associated with free time during the workday, refined manners, dress-up clothes, delicate food, fine china, and silver tea services and implements. By the mid-nineteenth century, the booming new silver-plating industry, plus the discovery of new silver deposits in Nevada, led to the proliferation of specialized silver pieces, many of them tea wares such as showy hot-water swing kettles, butter dishes, spoon holders, sugar tongs, cake baskets, and more.

Fund-raising tea parties of the nineteenth century, fancy events in which guests wore elaborate historical costumes, had also established an association between upper classes and tea. Parties to raise funds for the restoration of Mount Vernon and other venerable old buildings, for example, or to mark the one-hundredth anniversary of the Boston Tea Party, celebrated American history with style and pomp. After the centennial celebration of 1876 in Philadelphia, the popularity of tea drinking rose. In the early twentieth century, the very rich continued their love affair with tea, building private tea houses on their estates, in rustic twig cottages, Oriental pagodas with winged roofs, and vine-covered latticework pergolas.

The elite fund-raising tradition would live on in some of the public tea rooms and tea houses of the twentieth century. Alumnae of the Seven Sister colleges established tea rooms to raise funds for their alma maters. In Madison, New Jersey, alumnae of Wellesley College raised money at the Bottle Hill Tea Shop, while in Chicago, Vassar alums acted as hostesses at the Vassar House. Women of means interested in good works started tea rooms to aid their less fortunate sisters. Women's exchanges ran tea rooms and sold linens hand-embroidered by gentlewomen in financial distress. Handicraft associations were formed to give dignified employment to native American Indians and newly arrived immigrants.

But for most patrons, tea rooms were simply places to relax and have a good time. Although less connected to work and the business world, tea time in the early twentieth century was a lot like the cocktail hour of subsequent decades, a time to unwind, to "network," and to see and be seen. Tea in hotel tea rooms resembled the cocktail hour in another important way: customers sometimes passed up tea for alcoholic drinks. A journalist who followed three well-dressed women to a "fern-and-flower-decked" tea room after a "woman problem" play in 1913 wrote an insinuating critique of their drinking habits. He noted that a waiter served them the "special brand of tea ordered, the notable fact about which was that it failed to steam when poured." It was, however, consumed in teacups, which, along with the reporter's tone, made it clear that drinking by women was not considered fully acceptable. Hotel tea rooms were also battlegrounds for women who wanted to smoke, with many hotels forbidding women to light up while allowing men the privilege.

Afternoon tea was predominantly a female affair, but many women were joined by husbands and male friends and acquaintances, and tea often furnished an occasion for a romantic interlude. Frances Willard, a leader of the Woman's Christian Temperance Union, had observed in 1897 that afternoon tea rooms for society women were needed and that they "should be a lady's resort exclusively." But, in fact, few tea rooms excluded men, despite the fact that many restaurants barred women, a few continuing to do so into the 1960s.

Women's exclusion from many public dining rooms in the 1900s and 1910s was undoubtedly a factor in their attraction to female-friendly tea rooms. Most women were reluctant to challenge the widespread rule in hotels and fine dining rooms that unescorted women would not be served. Two women travelers in 1906 were embarrassed when the waiter in a New York City restaurant kept badgering them, asking, "When does your escort arrive?" "Escort?" they replied. "Your father, husband, brother?" he demanded. When they explained they were alone, he told them the table was engaged. The headwaiter then advised them "confidentially" that they could not eat there and they left, with "everybody watching us and wondering." Crossing the country by car in 1915, etiquette maven Emily Post and a female friend got the same treatment in a hotel they stayed at in Omaha. In the tea room, however, women were never turned away, at least not because of their gender. Social acceptability was another issue, particularly in the elite hotels.

High Season in the Hotel Tea Room

The hotel palm court was the place to be during the fall and winter social seasons of the 1910s, with half the crowd come to watch, said a British visitor, and the other half adorned in "gorgeous raiment who trail in to

Tea Room, Copley Plaza Hotel, Boston, Mass.

219949

TEA ROOM IN THE
COPLEY-PLAZA HOTEL
IN BOSTON, AROUND
1915.

reserved tables to be seen." Tables were set close together, separated only by a screen of plants, allowing for easy eavesdropping. The Plaza in New York opened in 1907. Its tea room, under a glass-domed ceiling, faced Fifth Avenue and was originally named the Tea Court. Tiny tables and delicate chairs (identical to those found in Boston's Copley Hotel) were arranged around the lofty marble pillars. The Copley and the Hotel Muehlebach Tea Foyer in Kansas City were likewise decorated with palms, as was the otherwise-named Laurel Court at the Fairmont Hotel in San Francisco. These were living palms, but the hotel wishing to save a few dollars could order artificial palms with leaves that could be removed for cleaning. The 1911 Albert Pick Company catalog insisted, "A number of these palms placed about the room give the exact appearance of a southern grove, with its silent invitation to rest and luxurious ease."

Evidently the Plaza met the requirements of at least one discerning British visitor in 1913. (Tea was something British tourists always checked out in America and usually complained bitterly about.) She found the Plaza acceptable, but the Manhattan Hotel was too full of "young girls and chappies from the schools." The Ritz Hotel and Sherry's Restaurant were too proper and dull, and the rest "more or less impossible," but she loved the giant palms and tiny tables at the Plaza.

The garden look, with luxurious profusions of flowers and plants, some strung from the ceilings, was so popular in this era that, according to the *New York Times* in March of 1910, "One hotel manager said that his flower bill was larger than his bill for the servants employed in the tea room." Wisteria, ferns, and smilax were also commonly used in hotel tea rooms. The Hotel Jefferson in St. Louis had a ceiling so draped with wisteria, it nearly brushed the heads of the Japanese servers. An Oriental motif was carried out in gilt bamboo-style chairs and red-and-white china tea sets. The Greenbrier in White Sulphur Springs, West Virginia, created a Wisteria Room, with living trees, a wisteria-draped ceiling, huge latticed windows, and garden statuary. Wicker furniture was often used to enhance the garden feeling, as was done at the Muehlebach and the Prince George Hotel in New York City, where vines appeared to halfway cover the

TEA AMONG THE PALMS, AT NEW YORK'S PLAZA HOTEL, CIRCA 1910.

TEA AT THE BLUE LANTERN INN

backlighted faux-glass ceiling. At the Menger in San Antonio, Texas, vines trailed up and over doorways and grew from wall sconces, while baskets of flowers adorned small tables throughout the series of spacious tea rooms. At the tea room of the Biltmore Ice Gardens in New York, guests sat on chairs covered in floral upholstery, amid ferns and vines, as they watched ice-skaters outside the plate-glass windows in winter. In summer an Italian sunken garden replaced the ice rink.

In Florida, no decorators were needed to create the much loved garden atmosphere. At the Royal Poinciana Hotel in Palm Beach, afternoon tea was served outdoors under the majestic (and very real) palm trees. Although they lacked palm trees, patrons of the Ritz-Carlton in New York were able to enjoy an outdoor Japanese tea garden. Announcing its opening June 1, 1917, the Ritz advertized in *Vanity Fair:* "This wonderfully unique out-of-doors restaurant with its stream of running water, its artistic pagodas, its exquisite rock and floral work and miniature bridges, all the work of leading Japanese artisans and landscape gardeners, is the accepted meeting place of society for Luncheon and Tea."

A wisteria "hanging garden" often complemented a Japanese motif in the early tea rooms. But even without the wisteria, Japanese themes were popular. The Homestead Hotel in Virginia Hot Springs used this, as did the Congress Hotel in Chicago, and the Peacock Tea Room in the Hotel Alexandria in Los Angeles. Shoji screens and lanternlike lighting were typically featured in Japanese tea rooms, but the Congress went one step further with a huge brass tea urn in the center of its tea room in 1907. Chinese touches were also popular. A copy of a gold-and-blue Chinese carpet and Chinese Chippendale furniture in "old blue lacquer" and covered in silk brocade decorated the tea room of the Hotel Pennsylvania, which was an extension of the main lobby. Ornate Chinese furnishings filled the pre-World War I tea room of the Hotel Osborn in Eugene, Oregon.

On nearby streets outside the big New York hotels, smaller tea rooms were opened, mostly by entrepreneurial women. As early as 1897, an Englishwoman named Kathryn P. Martyn ran a tea room at 291 Fifth Avenue, near the Waldorf-Astoria Hotel's original location. Beginning with only afternoon tea, she was soon begged by guests to furnish breakfast too. She also delivered delicate food to customers who were sick. Her crumpets were popular with American guests who had never tasted the real thing. In summers she ran her tea room in Newport, Rhode Island. Sallie M. Tucker operated a flower shop in New York City around 1900, across the street from the Waldorf. Finding she had more room than she needed, she put in a few tables for society women to meet and take light refreshments. Soon her tea room business crowded out the florist business, so she enlarged and developed into a tea room serving lunch à la carte and dinners from a fixed-price menu. Sallie Tucker also ran The Fernery Tea Cottage in Lakeville, Connecticut. Catering to high society meant following them to resort areas once the fall/winter season ended in the city, for there would be few elite patrons during summer in the city.

Mrs. Eva Duncan Kanevin, a widow, ran a fashionable place in the Loop in Chicago called The Delvies in 1917 and also managed hotel restaurants, most likely tea rooms. Mrs. Kanevin's employment by hotels is an indication of how eager these establishments were to attract women guests, because normally hotels were staffed almost exclusively by men, with few women employed outside of housekeeping. The Waldorf-Astoria hired Leonora Rector Crook, a member of Natchez, Mississippi, high society, to act as hostess in its Rose Room tea room in the 1920s. She also managed Sherry's tea room on Park Avenue.

Hotel tea rooms often held tea dances, featuring full orchestras, which became popular in the pre–World War I era. The usual rules were reversed and men were often not admitted unless accompanied by a woman. College students crowded the dance floors. At the Plaza, tea dancing began in 1912, and young people shocked their elders with "animal dances," which included not only the fox-trot, but also the bunny hug, grizzly bear, turkey trot, and kangaroo dip. Tea dances, fashionably known as thé dansants, became common around this time, but once national Prohibition started in 1920 these festive events became even more popular. In Washington, D.C., the Wardman Park Hotel arranged tables and chairs along the walls in its tea room, leaving the central corridor free for dancing. The American House in Boston converted their rathskeller into an afternoon tea and dancing venue. In June of 1920 they advertised afternoon tea dances (with tea and dancing for 75¢ per person) featuring a marimba band on Saturdays. Mr. and Mrs. Addison Fowler were on hand to give demonstrations of "Classic and Whirlwind dances." The dancing craze of the 1920s gave the afternoon tea habit a huge boost.

Elite Patrons

Just as they chose the best entertainment, tea rooms were careful to select their customers. A couple going for tea at the Plaza in 1913 noticed how the headwaiter "in an instant glance of steel-blue eyes decides that you are fit" before finding you a table. High prices were successful in keeping poor and working-class people out, but tea rooms took extra measures to keep other sorts of "the wrong people" away. In the teens this category of undesirables might have included people of Southern or Eastern European ethnicity, or those whose exuberance in dress or manner marked them as having bad taste. These were the people who allegedly patronized "lobster palaces," expensive but gaudy restaurants that attracted visitors to New York looking for a good time.

Then, as now, establishments used coded messages to appeal to their desired clientele. French in business names and menu terms was one type of signal. *Thé complet*, for instance, was not a meal meant for just anyone. Any place advertising that it was quiet or that it furnished dainty luncheons virtually shouted out that it was not for the masses. In 1916, the Colonia Tea Room proclaimed in *Vanity Fair* that it had "a quiet atmosphere that appeals to women of culture."

Steep prices were typical of elite tea rooms. Afternoon tea in an upscale hotel could easily cost as much as a whole dinner in a cheap restaurant. At the Copley Hotel tea room around 1910, for instance, a dish of figs alone cost 35¢. For that same amount, a customer in a Boston lunchroom could get a hot entrée, beverage, and dessert. A survey of single workingwomen in Boston in inflationary 1917 found that most could not afford a cafeteria meal that averaged out to 18¢.

Few people of color, regardless of their means, would have dared to enter a tea room unless it was specifically meant to cater to them, which—outside of Harlem—very few were. In Nella Larson's 1929 novel, *Passing*, the white-skinned protagonist, Irene Redfield, goes for tea on the roof of the "Drayton" in Chicago and experiences an anxious moment when she thinks she's been detected as a Negro. She fears she'll be asked to leave and imagines with steely realism "the polite and tactful way in which the Drayton would probably do it." Since she was passing, she would not have gone to an African-American tea room such as the Poro Beauty College's Poro Tea Room in Chicago, described in one guidebook as where "the wealthier class of colored people" dined and lunched. Nor would she have gone to the Duck Inn, also on South Parkway. There the hostess, Mrs. Elier Richardson, was black and so, presumably, were the patrons. On the whole though, black women, if found anywhere in the tea room, were most likely in the kitchen, cooking and cleaning up. A minority of tea rooms also employed black women as waitpersons. Beyond these positions, opportunities were limited. The Fanny Farmer cooking school in Boston offered a tea room training course in the 1920s and 1930s, but did not allow African-Americans to take it.

Recent immigrants would also have been unlikely to enjoy tea rooms or to have been welcomed in most of them. The cuisine in tea rooms was Anglo-American to the core. In a country where most turn-of-the-century restaurants were run by Europeans, with European-influenced French, German, or Hungarian dishes, the tea room ventured into unfamiliar territory. Most of the few ethnic Americans in the tea room business were northern-European Germans or Scandinavians who ran shops in the upper Midwest. Only a few tea rooms specialized in continental cuisine. During the 1940s, the Window Shop in Cambridge, Massachusetts, specializing in Viennese dishes, was run by two Austrians for the benefit of refugees in the United States; the Horvath Tea Room in Youngstown, Ohio, served Hungarian food; and the Brick School Tea House in Kinderhook, New York, served Viennese specialties and also made bread from stone-ground flour. But such places were rare.

Afternoon tea is itself an elite meal in that its delicacy and timing between lunch and dinner presumes an absence of hunger. A lettuce sandwich, costing 25¢ at the Hotel Cleveland's Tea Lounge in the early 1920s, could scarcely satisfy a hungry worker. Chicken salad might do better, but at 90¢ it cost as much as three meals. By the 1920s many tea rooms had expanded beyond afternoon tea and added lunch and dinner service. The tea room, announced one trade magazine, was "no longer a place of light afternoon refreshment for the idle rich." But many places still

THE COPLEY-PLAZA

Tea or Coffee 25
Cocoa 30   Chocolate 30
Demi Tasse 15
Clam Broth 40
Cup Consomme 40
French Pastry (each) 20   Napoleon 30
Petits Fours 40
Chivers Marmalade 30
Domestic Marmalade 30
Individual Figs 30
Assorted Jellies and Jams (each) 30
Small Tea Sandwiches 20
Melted Cheese on Toast 40
Dry or Butter Toast 25   English Muffins 15
Club Cheese Cracker 30   Cinnamon Toast 30
-: ICES :-
Lemon 45 Raspberry 45   Pineapple 45 Orange 45
Pistache 50   Chocolate 50   Vanilla 50
Coffee 50   Strawberry Parfait 60 Tutti-Frutti 60
Chocolate or Café Parfait 60   Biscuit Tortoni 60
Meringue-Glacée 60   Strawberry Ice Cream 50
Sultana Roll 60   Orangeade 40   Lemonade 30

COPLEY-PLAZA HOTEL
TEA MENU, CIRCA
1910.

aimed at elite patronage and did their best to draw it.

High prices were deemed advisable if a tea room wanted to stay exclusive. Advertising low prices was seen as a sure way to draw the wrong kind of customers. Mrs. S.D. Moore, of the Blue Lantern in Louisville, Kentucky, explained in 1922 that the "moneyed purse" was her desired client because she could not afford to cater to "the cafeteria or restaurant crowd." She kept her prices high to "eliminate the masses." The proprietor of a Cape Cod tea room said bluntly, in 1915, "People who stop and grumble at prices are usually not the desirable kind." The patrons must have agreed because one man wrote a comment in the guest book that ridiculed the Ford Motor Company's own advertising slogan: "Look at the price list and *watch the Fords go by.*" Tea and toast cost 35¢.

A subdued ambience achieved by dark colors and dim lighting was believed effective in keeping out "the commonplace, restless element" that liked the bright lights and hubbub of the glitzy cafés of 1908. Adopting furnishings found in "fine homes" was also recommended. Decor was carefully designed to convey signals of tasteful affluence. At the Wade Park Manor residential hotel in Cleveland, which catered to "an exclusive patronage," a long list of adjectives and proper names were attached to the objects in the Palm Room tea room: glazed faience tile flooring; a latticed wall with "Grinling Gibbons" picture frames; fancy furniture supplied by the Palmer and Embury Manufacturing Company of New York; a beamed ceiling; bronze decorations by the renowned Oscar B. Bach Studio in New York; Chinese vases on teakwood stands; a harewood console; and lights with parchment shades. A book kept in the kitchen recorded guests' special likes and dislikes, so that they did not have to reiterate their needs tiresomely. Residents ate in a fancy dining room and were not allowed to cook in their suites as the cooking smells might bother their neighbors.

In the 1920s, when the old guard believed all morals were being abandoned, a host of suggestions were made for keeping standards high in tea rooms. In 1922 cooking teacher Alice Bradley sternly warned tea room operators of the dangers of stale cake, soft butter balls, and cheap pictures on the wall, revealing perhaps how many mediocre tea rooms had sprung up in recent years. Some tea rooms sought remedies by dressing waitresses in conservative black-and-white uniforms, hiring society women as hostesses, sending invitations to the socially elect, and choos-

THE OLD ACADEMY TEA ROOM IN FAIRFIELD, CONNECTICUT, DISPLAYS THE TYPE OF ASCETIC INTERIOR FAVORED BY "PEOPLE OF GOOD TASTE" EARLY IN THE TWENTIETH CENTURY.

ing their tea room's name carefully. The Lone Pine Inn, located on a primary highway in the Midwest (a risky location), mailed cards to country-club members and avoided "promiscuous" advertising. They did not allow their inn *ever* to be referred to as a "roadhouse." A 1923 tea room correspondence course suggested that high-class tea rooms should choose names like White Peacock or Silver Pheasant, which suggested fashionable or smart atmosphere. Do not use unattractive names like Tubbs' or Blodgett's or silly names like Kill Kare or Dew Come Inn, said another tea room expert.

Gentlewomen Proprietors

Hotel tea rooms were managed by men, for the most part. But the small, independent tea rooms that began in the 1910s were usually owned, operated, and fully staffed by women, oftentimes middle-class women. Those in the tea room business believed that it took "a gentlewoman to run a successful tea room," a notion that was closely allied with the belief that only a lady of refinement could—or should—make a salad.

Despite the fact that tea rooms were intended to preserve the social class hierarchy, they still managed to bring about a remarkable occupational shift in American society. For the first time, college-educated Anglo-Saxons—women all—ventured into the hospitality field. They were quite daring because the restaurant business was considered by this class, which despised saloons and generally supported temperance, to be "the tail end of the saloon business." Grace E. Smith, who in 1918 opened the Ottawa Hills Tea House, in an elite suburb of Toledo, Ohio, said her family was ashamed to see her enter the restaurant business after she graduated

DELICATE TEATIME TREATS

Lettuce Sandwiches, Greenwich Tea Room, Connecticut

Orange Straws, Marshall Field & Company, Chicago

Cream Cheese and Walnut Sandwich on Raisin Bread,
New York Exchange for Woman's Work

Cheese Dreams, Sevillia, New York

Olive Sandwiches, Hotel Cleveland Tea Lounge

Waffles and Maple Syrup, The Colonia, New York

Pineapple Charlotte, Miss Ellis Tea Room, Chicago

Cream Cheese with Ginger Sandwiches, Maillard,
New York

TEA SANDWICHES RECOMMENDED FOR TEA ROOMS. *TOP:* **ROUND SANDWICHES WITH CENTERS OF JELLY.** *BOTTOM:* **CHECKERBOARD SANDWICHES OF WHITE AND WHOLE WHEAT.**

Hot Gingerbread, Afternoon Tea-Room, Fifth Avenue, New York

Welsh Rarebit, Ocean House, Swampscott, Massachusetts

Hartford Election Cake, Old Hundred, Southbury, Connecticut

Creamed Sweetbreads on Toast, F&R Lazarus & Co. Tea Room, Columbus, Ohio

Cinnamon Toast, Nobleboro Community Kitchen, Nobleboro, Maine

Cheese and Date Butter Sandwich, Empire Room, Waldorf-Astoria, New York

Southern Beaten Biscuits with Honey, Blue Parrot Inn, Denver

Grilled Sardines on Toast with Asparagus Tips, College Inn, Sherman House, Chicago from Wooster College in 1908. "In those days, many of the restaurants were either cafés with liquor service or were the cheap lunchrooms," she reflected in 1940.

At the top of the restaurant trade, when Grace E. Smith entered the business, were the German-trained hotelmen who ran everything by the book, managing their kitchens and dining rooms with military precision. Although fly-ridden lunchrooms serving simple fare were commonplace, most eating places of any pretension had a distinct European flavor, and menus were frequently written in French. American restaurant cuisine was a sui generis conglomeration, influenced by a European past but unidentifiable as belonging to any particular nation, and mainly known—and disliked—for its sauces, which middle-class Anglo-Americans were convinced disguised spoiled meat. Often menus were chosen from a yearly book, repeated faithfully every 365 days (if not more often). Meat predominated, and fresh salads and vegetables played a minor role. Apart from managers, most restaurant personnel were recent male immigrants with little formal education. At high-class restaurants they dressed in black tuxedolike uniforms that Anglo-Americans felt were food-stained and filthy. Alcoholic beverages were important in the profit makeup, and the restaurant business was closely tied to the alcohol industry, if not the saloon. As the slogan "wine, women, and song" connotes, eating out had a somewhat risqué tinge and was not considered appropriate for respectable men, much less women, except under special circumstances.

College-educated Anglo-American males would no more have entered the restaurant business than they would have sold newspapers on the corner. And yet, via the tea room and other small eating establishments, their sisters ventured in. Somehow the tea room was seen as quite separate and different from the restaurant, perhaps because it served no alcohol and catered primarily to women. Female college students also worked in tea rooms as waitresses, another phenomenon worth noting at a time that waitresses were (unfairly) considered virtual prostitutes in society's eyes. The manager and all her assistants at the tea room of Ocean House in Massachusetts were "college women," according to a 1922 report.

Put in the context of the prevailing hospitality industry of turn-of-the-twentieth-century America, it seems astonishing that two young society women were irresistibly drawn to running a tea room in 1897. Elizabeth Vanderpoel Duer, of "Hauxhurst," in Weehawken Heights, New Jersey, and her friend Gertrude Houghton, daughter of the rector of Trinity Church in Hoboken, opened a resort tea room in Greenwich, Connecticut, for summer residents and bicyclists. They rented a room and decorated it with pink-and-white wallpaper and dotted-swiss curtains and created a menu of ice cream, cake, tongue, ham, and chicken sandwiches, and specialty drinks of café frappé and café mousse. They, of course, had little idea of the immense appeal their venture would have to later generations of women, particularly in the 1920s when the desire to have a tea room mushroomed into an absolute craze.

By the 1920s it was almost commonplace for upper-class women to enter the restaurant industry, usually via tea rooms. An example is Mrs. Katherine H. Talbot, who spoke to the National Restaurant Association at their annual meeting in 1926, with an address titled "Atmosphere and Refinement in Restaurant Operation." She was a patron of the arts and the widow of a General Motors executive. Upon his death, "as a mere pastime," she opened a tea room called The Grey Manor in her grandfather's home in Dayton, Ohio. Then, after deciding to focus all her energies on the tea room, she built it into an establishment known throughout the Midwest as "a place of quality and refinement."

The college-educated and middle- and upper-class women brought a whole new set of tastes and values to tea rooms and small tea room restaurants. Since men would not work under the command of a woman, the owners had little choice but to hire all-women staffs—quite a novelty. They brought recipes from home, many of them for simple yet refined dishes with French parentage, for French cookery had become fashionable with affluent Americans in the 1870s, when adoption of French terms from *bouillon* to *soufflé* caught on. Their cooking often interpreted the English tradition through a French filter, producing more delicate and elegant results. For the brown sauces of traditional restaurant cookery they substituted cream sauces. They introduced patties, salads, and light desserts made without the European pastry chef's sometimes artificial flamboyance.

Many of the "new women" tea room proprietors scorned the too ornate decor of the hotel, opting instead for the decidedly anti-Victorian and upscale "Craftsman" style made famous by the English Arts & Crafts movement and by Kate Cranston's fabulously stylish Willow Tea Rooms in Glasgow, Scotland, designed in part by Charles Rennie Mackintosh. In America, many of the early independent tea rooms had the signature Arts & Crafts look of bare floors and tabletops, Mission furniture, exposed brick walls and ceiling beams, wainscoting topped by decorative friezes, and hanging lights and sconces, frequently adjoined by vine-covered porches, pergolas, and piazzas for outdoor eating (another innovation). The Arts and Crafts Cottage and Tea Garden in Edgartown, Massachusetts, for instance, was run by two women of taste in 1910. It sold hand-decorated china and Craftsman jewelry and baskets, along with afternoon tea and sandwiches made to order for sailing parties.

Although writers such as F. Scott Fitzgerald have portrayed wealthy Americans of this period as enamored of opulence, tea room patrons were from another cultural milieu, one that rejected excessive decoration and fanciness. They preferred instead the austerity of "reform" styles such as Arts & Crafts and Colonial Revival. Alice Puffer ran a simple summer tea

room in Nobleboro, Maine, with her two sisters, attracting a wealthy clientele of Bar Harbor millionaires, many of whom arrived in limousines driven by uniformed chauffeurs. She noted, "I believe that the very modesty of our little place attracted the best type of tourists and cottagers."

Many tea rooms also shared in common with the Arts & Crafts movement an emphasis on handmade decorative appointments, Japanese and Native American Indian designs and objects, and rustic furniture. So many tea rooms used the handwoven rag rugs in small block and check patterns made by E.C. Beetem & Sons of Carlisle, Pennsylvania, that this style of carpet was called by the name Tea Room. These rugs, which combined beautifully with Craftsman furniture, were based on Colonial designs that Beetem started using at the time of the 1876 centennial. In combining these rugs with Craftsman and Colonial furnishings, tea rooms showed the crossover of Arts & Crafts and Colonial Revival styles in the pre–World War I period.

❖ ❖ ❖

Despite all its luxury, refinement, and high-class representations—or maybe *because* of these qualities—the tea room was about to be rocketed out of its complacent niche by the tea room proprietors of Greenwich Village just about the same time college students started doing the kangaroo dip at the Plaza. The Village's tea rooms would add a layer of complexity to tea room history that would vastly enrich it, make it more fun, and democratize it (at least a little bit). Afterward, there would be two kinds of tea rooms: the proper bourgeois kind and the not-so-proper bohemian kind. The tea room craze was about to take a walk on the wild side.

CHAPTER TWO

Village Bohemian

It is the young women who open most of the studios, run most of the tearooms and restaurants, most of the little art shops and book stalls, manage the exhibits and little theaters, dominate the life of the bohemias of American cities.

—*THE GOLD COAST AND THE SLUMS*, 1929

Women made their mark in Greenwich Village before the First World War. Many who lived there were social workers at area settlement houses, teachers, and reformers. They were committed professionals, but they were also social rebels interested in loosening the Victorian restrictions of the time. Around 1910 they were joined by artists, both male and female, who began moving to the Village to take advantage of its attractive ambience and low rents, with additional waves of expatriates from Paris coming in before 1914 as war threatened to break out in Europe. This interesting mix, along with growing ranks of writers, radicals, feminists, and "ultramodern" couples, produced a lively, fun-seeking culture, with plenty of clubs, salons, and tea rooms to hang out in.

Tea rooms in the Village were modeled on Paris's Latin Quarter, as were many of the lifestyles and customs of this period. Villagers lived in tiny furnished rooms, spending so much of their time in clubs and tea rooms they would often give them for their address. Everyone kept unusual hours, often staying up all night, and eating breakfast at 5 P.M. Some tea rooms accommodated these odd habits, such as the Black Parrot, whose hours were 8:30 P.M. to 1 A.M., and another that advertised, "Open all night and frequently during the day."

As described by cultural historian Carolyn Ware, the Village was a place "where flourished free love, unconventional dress, erratic work—if any—indifference to physical surroundings, all-night parties, crowding, sleeping where one happened to be, walking the streets in pajamas, girls on the street smoking, plenty of drink, [and] living from moment to moment." In 1922, *Vanity Fair* characterized Greenwich Village as a place of "Batiks, Art Students, Tea-Rooms, and free verse poets." During the 1920s, as its fame spread, Americans from Brooklyn, New Jersey, Kalamazoo, and just about everywhere else became fascinated with it. For better or worse, the Village would become recognized as "the cradle of modern American culture." Writer Joseph Freeman, who lived in the Village in this period, observed that prosperous middle-class America needed Greenwich Village bohemianism to learn to "spend their money in ways not sanctioned by the puritan tradition."

And there were many delightful ways to spend money impulsively in Greenwich Village. Most of what was sold were imported goods or locally handmade items, since Villagers had no love for the wares of industrial America. Often run in tandem with tea rooms were enterprises selling batik clothing, hand-painted bead necklaces, cigarette holders, imported wares from Holland, hand carvings, pottery, and art prints. Dorothy Benjamin, wife of world-famous opera singer Enrico Caruso, ran the Treasure Chest gift shop with two male friends. The photographs of Jessie Tarbox Beals, now renowned as the first woman news photographer, were sold there. Shops with too cute names such as Washington Squares sold fudge, while the Tart Mart presumably sold pastries, and the Bazaar de Junk peddled antiques. Kraftwoven, sharing an address on West Eighth Street with the Penguin Book Shop, was one of several weaving studios in the early 1920s and featured "stunning polychromatic weaving" and "the smartest sport and street clothes in the city." A surprisingly large number of craftspeople made lamps and lampshades, perhaps reflecting the transition from gas to electric lighting under way.

Often the gift shops were run inside tea rooms, along with so many other activities that the core identity of a business might be hard to classify. In 1917 the New York Times noted that one tea room advertised "drinks that are different, open fires, gifts, pictures, exhibitions of painting, ukulele instructions, batik gowns, costumes, scarfs, hats, bags, and negligees designed and made to order." In 1922, T.N.T. publicized the following activities, amenities, and attributes: "Cozy—Dancing—1 A.M.—Dinners—Table d'hôte—Dreams—à la Carte—Unique—Liberal—Clubby—Chess—Music—1 A.M.—Fun—Talk—Tea—Talk—Coffee—Afternoons—Village—Cheer—Gossip—Food—1 A.M.—Atmosphere—Bridge—Ideas—Recreation—Comfort—Fireplace—Art—Cigarettes—Smocks—Laughter—Checkers—Parties—Personalities—Service—Seclusion—Bohemia—Song—1 A.M." In 1925, the Queen of Hearts offered candies, tea, books, and crossword puzzles. Gifts were also peddled by strolling merchants such as Sonia the cigarette girl and Tiny Tim, a maker of "soul" candies wrapped in paper scribbled with his poetry.

Greenwich Village denizen and writer Floyd Dell attributed the genesis of the modern, bohemian Greenwich Village to socialist-feminist schoolteacher Henrietta Rodman. After a disagreement with other members of the rather conservative uptown Liberal Club, Rodman moved her cadre of university students, professors, newspapermen and -women, and social workers to the Village in 1913. Realizing a restaurant would help pay the rent, the club hired Polly Holladay from Chicago to run one in the club's basement. Polly's, as it was known, soon became the heart of the Village, creating a sense of community. Polly's was originally on Washington Place, later the site of the Dutch Oven tea room. It was filled with colorfully painted tables and a spirited crowd who spent hours debating social issues. Strictly speaking, Polly's was not a tea room since it served red wine—a Village staple beverage before, after, and during Prohibition—but in spirit it was not at all unlike the tea rooms that would spring up around it in the years to come. Polly's financial success inspired many other women to open small tea rooms in the neighborhood, and a scene was born.

"We're All Mad Here"

The Mad Hatter, with an *Alice in Wonderland* theme, was one of the earliest tea rooms in the Village, established around 1916 by sculptor Edith Unger. The Mad Hatter was located behind the Pepper Pot on West Fourth, and beneath the Samovar. It made the most of its inconspicuous basement

MAP DRAWN IN 1926 BY BOBBY EDWARDS, EDITOR OF *THE QUILL*, A GREENWICH VILLAGE MAGAZINE
OF HUMOR AND OPINION. TEA ROOMS SHOWN ON THE MAP INCLUDE THE CRUMPERIE, WASHINGTON
SQUARE TEA SHOP, THE BLUE HORSE, THE MAD HATTER, THE KOPPER KETTLE, PIG 'N WHISTLE,
ROMANY MARIE'S, ALICE MCCOLLISTER'S, THE JUMBLE SHOP, AND THE HEARTHSTONE.

entryway by inscribing "Eloh tibbar eht nwod" along the basement steps, leaving guests to decipher the puzzling inscription. Once inside, patrons saw scrawled on the walls "We're All Mad Here—I'm Mad, You're Mad, You Must Be or You Wouldn't Have Come Here" and knew for sure they were in for a good time.

Romany Marie's, started in 1912 by Marie Marchand, predated the Mad Hatter by several years and may have preceded Polly's as well. Like most tea rooms in the Village (though never officially called that—it too probably served wine), hers moved to new locations repeatedly. Marie was a native of Moldavia and frequently dressed in Gypsy clothing, read tea leaves, and affected, at times, a strong Romanian accent. She was known to be an associate of famed anarchist Emma Goldman, who was deported to the Soviet Union during the Red Scare purges of 1920.

Although Marie distanced herself from anarchism, she retained an abiding interest in the designs of utopian visionaries. Visionary architect and designer Buckminster Fuller made a few pieces of furniture in 1928 to decorate her restaurant in Minetta Lane in exchange for free meals. He said of Marie's, at a time when many claimed the Village had been commercialized beyond recognition, that it reminded him of Paris and was "loaded...with great artists and great intellectuals." In 1929, Marie and her business partner, Ariel "Puck" Durant (wife of philosopher Will Durant), gave Fuller space in their restaurant, now moved to a basement in South Washington Square, to display a model of his futuristic Dymaxion House and to lecture on it. Other well-known guests of Romany Marie's included Eudora Welty, who went there when she was a student in advertising at Columbia Business School in 1930, and best-selling author Fanny Hurst, a regular. Romany Marie was a dynamic character in bohemian Greenwich Village, and a vivid portrait of her, painted by John Sloan, is now part of the Whitney Museum's permanent collection.

By 1917 there were enough tea rooms in the Village to cause the *New York Times* to remark that the Village was a place "whose inhabitants make their living by keeping restaurants for each other." Another tea room of the first wave was the Samovar, run by Nanni Bailey, who also acted in her brother-in-law's Provincetown Theater play "Not Smart" (local Provincetown slang for getting pregnant out of wedlock). Others included the Will o' the Wisp, the Mouse Trap, the Candlestick, Back Home (with a rural mailbox for its sign), the Idee Chic, Ye Silhouette Shop, Camouflage, My Tea Wagon, the Crumperie, the Dragon Fly, the Little Sea Maid, and the Pig 'n Whistle. (Clever names were to become one of the Village's major exports.) At least six tea shops were found in one four-story building on Sheridan Square: the Aladdin Shop, the Russian Tea Room (not to be confused with the famous restaurant formerly on West Fifty-seventh), Romany Marie's, the Pirates' Den, the Black Parrot, and the Vermillion Hound.

The number of tea rooms continued to grow after the war. In March 1920, a story in *Ladies' Home Journal* said there were "never so many tea rooms" in the Village. "It sometimes seems as if every Villager were extended the privilege of an individual eating place," wrote Corinne Low, herself a Villager and convinced that readers in a "little Montana mining town" would not believe the world of independent women and men she was describing was real.

Would not believe it—or would not accept it? As was true of the tea rooms of swank hotels in the decade before Greenwich Village tea rooms blossomed, the Village's tea room owners and customers were mostly a privileged group, mainly college-educated, white Protestants from comfortable backgrounds in New England and the Midwest. As was true of

THROUGH THE ALLEY UP THE STAIRS AND OVER THE ROOF AT
148 WEST FOURTH STREET
Greenwich Village   Phone Spring 7927

ADVERTISEMENTS FROM 1919 FOR THE SAMOVAR AND THE BLACK PARROT TEA SHOPS IN GREENWICH VILLAGE.

MISS CRUMP SERVES CRUMPETS

In addition to crumpets, Mary Alletta Crump served "crumpled" eggs, toasted sponge cake, pea soup, and peanut butter sandwiches. Her first Crumperie tea shop opened in 1916 at 6 1/2 Sheridan Square, staying there briefly and then moving five times. A Smith College graduate originally from Virginia, Mary Alletta—known as Crumpy—was assisted in her venture by her mother, who baked crumpets and stirred her famous pea soup in a miniature kitchenette behind a curtain. Except for the first location in Sheridan Square, in a former harness shop next occupied by photographer Jessie Tarbox Beals, the two always lived over the shop.

Crumpy serenaded guests on her ukelele, playing Southern folk songs and Negro spirituals she had entertained the troops with during the First World War. Among her guests were artists, poets, actors, and writers, including Eugene O'Neill, Sinclair Lewis, Edna St. Vincent Millay ("a regular"), and Vachel Lindsay. Many of her guests were associated with the nearby Greenwich Village Theater. The Three Hours for Lunch Club, a literary club organized by Christopher Morley, a founder of the *Saturday Review*, met at the Crumperie.

According to Crumpy, socialists were not given a warm welcome at the Crumperie. When "radicals" came in, she recorded, "my mother, on observing the outfits and perhaps dirty shirts and nails, would serve 'em coldish coffee and perhaps an over done burnt crumpet, they'd leave complaining and seldom returned." They always wondered what people saw in the Crumperie, she said.

Although George Bernard Shaw never visited the Crumperie, Crumpy believed he had recommended it to English visitors, telling them it served "real" tea and crumpets. Crumpy later confessed, however, that when she heard a guest with an English accent enter her shop, she would cut open the tea bags she normally used.

The last Crumperie, the only one outside the Village, closed in 1926. Crumpy then worked for a while at the Grenfell Mission in Labrador and taught tea room management at a school in Brooklyn. In 1958 she won $16,000 on TV's *$64,000 Question*.

From the Crumperie guest book:

"The Crumperie has the Purple Pup and the Pink Nightmare pushed off the board."

—HAROLD VERMILYEA, A HOLLYWOOD ACTOR OF THE 1940S

"To a very charming Mother and daughter who have the most adorable tea place in the world." —PEGGY HOPKINS

"I ate here, got enough to eat and liked it." (Crumpy: "What an appetite he had.")

—HENDRIK WILLEM VAN LOON

"Tea at 'The Crumperie' has spoiled me forever for tea at Sherry's or the Ritz."

—DOROTHY COIT SPOONER, "A 1918 DEBUTANTE"

"Food is my only lust."

—EDNA ST. VINCENT MILLAY

LEFT: **INTERIOR OF THE CRUMPERIE AT ONE OF ITS MANY ADDRESSES, WITH THE PROPRIETOR SHOWN WEARING HER INVARIABLE APRON COSTUME** (photograph by Jessie Tarbox Beals). *(Smith College Archives, Smith College)*

RIGHT: **THE HOMEY IMAGE OF CRUMPY WAS FREQUENTLY USED FOR POSTCARDS AND MAGAZINES.**

1960s hippies, it is probable that many Americans disapproved of the values and lifestyles of the free-living Villagers, a number of whom were gay, "pagans," or advocates of pacifism and socialism. Several tea rooms experienced vandalism at the hands of their ethnic Italian and Irish neighbors. At least one Italian father from the neighborhood discovered his daughter in a tea room and made quite a scene as he ordered her out.

What ethnic and rural Americans thought about the Village had little bearing on its overall popularity, however. By 1923, someone observed there were so many tea rooms that "you may dine at a new place every night for weeks on end." Carolyn Ware estimated that forty was a conservative estimate of how many tea rooms were in business at any one time in the early 1920s. Village jester and editor of *The Quill*, Bobby Edwards, quipped, "In the Village everyone has two businesses—her neighbor's and a tea room."

The Lure of "Atmosphere"

If Greenwich Village tea rooms did not actually invent atmosphere, they certainly made it a highly desirable commodity. Tea room proprietors were well aware that this was what the public craved. According to writer Floyd Dell, uptowners were willing to "pay dear" for it. A 1925 advertisement by Romany Marie, for instance, proclaimed that her eatery, newly moved to 170 1/2 Waverly Place, had "more space, more air—but the same atmosphere." Villagers demonstrated a special flair for creating atmosphere as they transformed run-down tenement rooms into exotic locales for adventure and pleasure, sometimes simply by the magic of vibrant paint and candlelight.

An atmospheric interior was a solution to small budgets and cramped basement and attic spaces. Several tea rooms were awkwardly located in former stables or makeshift workshops. Visitors to the Samovar in 1919 were instructed to go "through the alley, up the stairs, and over the roof" to reach the entrance. One Samovar guest was convinced she had come to a warehouse by mistake. Once inside, though, she was enchanted with the whitewashed brick walls and the exposed rafters painted red. Employing the same improvisational decorating techniques they used in their living spaces, tea room owners diverted the eye from interior faults with color, lighting, and clever displays of attractive handcrafted objects. The tiny tea shop that photographer Jessie Tarbox Beals ran briefly in the summer of 1917 used barrels for tables, with bright tablecloths thrown over them and vases of flowers plunked down in the middle. In Jessie's own three-room flat, she and her roommate painted the walls turquoise and the furniture orange and black.

Many old buildings in the Village were tenements with unplastered brick walls and exposed pipes running across the ceilings. Tea room owners left the walls as they were, with the exposed brick taking on a new-found attractiveness that remains appealing today. They left pipes undisguised, suspending from them shawls, lanterns, or any manner of object. At the Pepper Pot, in a four-story building on West Fourth Street whose top floor housed the studio of retired silent-screen actress Viola Sherlock, red-hot peppers and Chinese lanterns were strung from a labyrinth of pipes. Although the Pepper Pot was big enough to accommodate two dance floors, most tea shops were small, and Village tour guide Adele Kennedy found she had to break large tours into groups of twenty to squeeze into them. Proprietors made the most of close quarters by dividing off improvised kitchen areas and work spaces with screens or exotic-patterned curtains.

Brightly painted interiors became a tea room hallmark. Rooms with green walls and violet ceilings might be filled with cadmium-yellow tables, boldly violating the standards of bourgeois "good taste." The new fascination with futuristic color combinations was due to the return of expatriate American artists from the Left Bank before the First World War. The splashiest colors were the most admired. Orange became so closely associated with Village tea rooms that one Villager with orange curtains frequently had tourists knocking on her door in 1920, certain her apartment was a tea shop. The Wigwam, a nightclubby tea room with entertainment by pseudo-Indian maidens, was painted by an artist who chose gray for the walls and orange for the ceiling.

But not all Greenwich Village tea rooms had futuristic color schemes. Many interiors were plainer and more sedate, and some even used Colonial motifs. Yet these too managed to achieve a high degree of artsiness, frequently by having talented patrons draw on the walls. Author Hendrik Willem Van Loon, husband of the Mad Hatter's second owner "Jimmie" Criswell, wrote his best-selling *The Story of Mankind* in the tea room. During writing breaks he sketched on the wall illustrations he would use in the book. Van Loon also painted murals on the walls of the Crumperie. Modernist painter Guy Pène du Bois created murals at the Jumble Shop. The most infamous murals, however, were done by a seventeen-year-old artist, Clara Tice. When she drew athletic nude women and human-sized insects on the wall of Polly's in 1914, retired captain of the Society for the Suppression of Vice Anthony Comstock personally arrived to order them destroyed. The incident made Tice famous and she was sought after as a book and magazine illustrator for years to come. ("He was some press agent," she said later of Comstock.)

The candle became a Village symbol. Poets read by their flickering light, and the Pirates' Den and the Wigwam had no other lighting, making them very denlike indeed. The Will o' the Wisp was normally so dim that it was hard to see at all. One day a patron arrived to find the place surprisingly lit up. The attendant jumped up, embarrassed, and turned off the lights. "I'm so sorry," she said, "but I wanted to *see* just a moment." The motto of the Mad Hatter, known more familiarly as the Rabbit Hole, was "cake, coffee, and candlelight." Like the Pepper Pot, candles at the Mad Hatter were allowed to drip onto their bases. At the Pepper Pot, artists were invited to carve candles with drippings that had accumulated over five years into sculptures of nudes, a favorite artistic subject in the neighborhood.

Celebrity Spotting

However much patrons may have been attracted to tea rooms' weird atmosphere, clearly this was secondary to seeing the Villagers themselves. Village tour guide Adele Kennedy, who once escorted three hundred club women from Bayonne, New Jersey, acknowledged in 1917 that tourists "come down here to see freaks." The natives' freedom, their zaniness, plus their penchant for discussing sex openly—and constantly—was a lure to repressed Americans from all over.

The "natives" were colorful to see and certainly looked different from the folks back home. Long hair was popular with men, and short hair for women. Men wore orange neckties, corduroys, and velvet sculptor's caps, while women wore artist's smocks with flowing ties, tam-o'-shanters, and sandals. Often Villagers went barefoot, although tour guide Adele Kennedy said she eventually had to abandon this practice because of debris from the subway construction. Informality ruled the day, and dressing up—except at gaudy costume parties—was unfashionable. (Costume balls were so popular that the Village supported at least three costume-design studios in 1919.)

Village artists and poets, in particular, personified the qualities visitors sought. Before rock and film stars, they were the celebrities. One tea room advertised in *Vanity Fair* in 1922: "Sixty Washington Square South. Home of famous artists. Here one finds delicious food and the charm of old New York. Take bus for luncheon, tea or dinner." Grace's Garret acquired a reputation as a place to meet poets and Bolsheviks. At the Greenwich Village Inn (Polly's reincarnated into a nightclub with a jazz band), patrons learned they might enjoy spontaneous entertainment from its "distinguished patronage." One wonders if tourists might have been disappointed at times, given that many Village natives were accustomed to playing bridge, chess, or other innocent games in tea rooms. Author Theodore Dreiser, for instance, had once joined a group of artists, poets, actresses, and editors in a tea room for the guessing game Up Jenkins, which continued noisily for hours until dawn. Bridge players, including playwright Eugene O'Neill and author Sinclair "Red" Lewis, filled the Mad Hatter. One wit said in 1926 that 110 percent of tea room customers were bridge players.

Some of the more commercially inclined Villagers saw to it that outsiders left with their wishes gratified. At the Pirates' Den, a crew of rowdies staged seemingly realistic fights. "Spontaneous" poetry recitals took place at what some said were "pseudo" tea rooms. Poet Eli Siegel, whose poem "Hot Afternoons Have Been in Montana" won a magazine contest and brought him fame, entertained customers by banging on tables and throwing dishes as he read Vachel Lindsay's anticapitalist poem "The Congo." Bobby Edwards, who edited the Village's entertainment guide *The Quill* and made ukuleles out of cigar boxes, was known to stroll around the Mad Hatter strumming and reciting his comical verses, such as "Because she wasn't cautious, the poor girl became nauseous, Allah be merciful!" In some places, it was alleged, young women were hired to impersonate artists' models, the sex symbols of their day.

A visit to a Village tea room in the 1920s nevertheless proved effective in relaxing the gentry's inhibitions. A party of about fifty Macy's employees and friends "making merry at a choice little tea room" in the Village in December of 1926 found the atmosphere just right. The group danced to an orchestra and "all barriers of reserve and the like were broken down, and self expression reigned supreme," recorded one of the revelers. Especially memorable to many of the Macy's employees was the sight of their bosses doing "Charleston exhibitions."

From Tea Room to Nightclub and Speakeasy

Romany Marie's continued to thrive into the 1940s, and the Jumble Shop carried on into the 1960s, although it opened a bar when Prohibition ended in the 1930s. Tea rooms that served no alcohol were still to be found at the end of the 1920s, but the Village's tea room phase began to lose momentum in 1923 when the New York legislature voted to discontinue funds for enforcing the liquor ban. Then speakeasies and nightclubs took over as the prime attractions for visitors to the Village. Floyd Dell criticized the philistine outsiders who came looking for "naughtiness,"

ended up staring at each other, "and think they are seeing life." As tourists flooded in, the locals moved away or retreated into quieter hangouts. The Fir Tree Inn claimed that its menus were prepared by a skilled chef and that "there is no attempt here to serve atmosphere instead of good food." At the Jumble Shop, guests were served good food "without submitting to entertainment." Helen Page, proprietor of one of the more subdued tea rooms, the Silhouette, opened another place on Ninth Street near Fifth Avenue that had no name, not even a sign. Tea rooms did not disappear, but those the locals patronized shed their bohemian trappings.

Other places that had once billed themselves as tea rooms went in the opposite direction, heightening their bohemian atmosphere to appeal to outsiders. The Pirates' Den, which had called itself a tea room of sorts early on, became a nightclub, and owner Don Dickerman opened up two additional clubs, the Blue Horse and the County Fair. The 4 Trees, at 4 Christopher Street, advertised in 1924 that it had "Glamour-Charm-Romance" and was "the smartest downtown rendez-vous for dining and dancing." The Jolly Friars Inn offered entertainment consisting of musical reviews by "colored collegians." In October of 1923 the Yellow Fan, the Blue Bird, and the Witch Cat were raided, liquor was found, and arrests were made.

Greenwich Village, Floyd Dell's "Coney Island of the Soul," was infamous as a "crazy place" by the mid-1920s. By that time it had probably received more national publicity than all the cities of the Midwest and South put together. It was featured in newspapers in large cities and small towns alike, in magazines as varied as *Vanity Fair* and the *Ladies' Home Journal*, and in travel guidebooks. The Village was pictured in movies such as *Within the Cup*, in 1918, about Tea-Cup Ann, who read fortunes in a tea room, and in other film scenes with tea rooms named the Black Beetle and the Purple Guinea Pig. Rows of tour buses parked in Washington Square, and Grace Godwin advertised in 1919 that her "Garret" was "opposite where the bus stops." The Pepper Pot was an "official stop" on the Gray Line tours: for $2.50 visitors in 1927 could take the "Grand Evening Tour" of the Gay White Way and the Bowery, dropping in there for refreshments.

Those Villagers who had belonged to the "genuine" days when the Liberal Club flourished were quick to condemn the commercialization of the mid-1920s. Oddly enough, they too had been judged in much the same way in 1917 by a visitor to Polly's, who thought everyone exhibited "excessive animation and vivacity." According to her, despite Polly's "overworked functionary with socialistic tendencies [probably waiter/chef Hippolyte Havel, who was known to call customers "bourgeois pigs"], excellent cooking, and moderate prices," the restaurant was out of keeping with the "real, inner life of the Village." Perhaps Hippolyte was right: the real Greenwich Village had never existed except in the imagination and was nothing but what he called "a state of mind."

Other Bohemias, Other Tea Rooms

Although Greenwich Village was the nation's largest and best-known bohemia—and the one with the most impact on the development of the tea room—it was not the only center of subcultural rebellion. Areas drawing unconventional poets, artists, writers, and others seeking refuge from mainstream "Babbittry" appeared all over the United States from around the turn of the century up until the mid-1920s.

Since 1894, with the publication of the best-selling novel of an artists' model, *Trilby* by George Du Maurier, a taste for bohemianism had gripped the imagination of thousands of Americans, women in particular. There had, in fact, been women artists sculpting and painting in Greenwich Village studios since 1895, in the pre-tea-room phase when bohemians had hung out in the area's "red ink places," Italian restaurants. In other cities as far-flung as San Antonio, Cincinnati, and Oakland, California, people had started bohemian clubs and periodicals. In Fort Worth, Texas, Mrs. Henry Clay Gorman established a bohemian reading room with an attached dining room and produced a magazine around 1898, the publication staying alive until 1904.

San Francisco's bohemia, catered to by French and Italian cafés, seemed to be populated mainly by men. Women, though, were more in evidence in Carmel, San Francisco's post-earthquake 1906 offshoot. By the 1920s Carmel had sprouted tea rooms with such names as Cabbages and Kings, the Studio, and the Bluebird. Around Copley Square in Boston circa 1918 was Nan's Kitchen, a tea room with two locations, one in a basement at 38 Huntington and the other at 10 Oxford Terrace. At the Huntington Avenue Nan's, the proprietor, who wore a smock, bloomers, and a tam, decorated her basement tea room with stenciled parrots, black cats, and maxims on the wall. Washington, D.C.'s Brick Wall Inn was described in 1928 as "the Greenwich Village of Washington," suggesting that city's alternative culture was minuscule indeed. It is likely that all major cities of the Northeast, Midwest, and Southwest, perhaps even the South, had small bohemian areas where galleries, little theaters, and tea rooms flourished, but evidence of this is hard to find today.

NAN'S KITCHEN AT 10 OXFORD TERRACE, COPLEY SQUARE, BOSTON, AROUND 1920. THE FIGURE AT THE RIGHT MAY BE NAN GURNEY, THE TEA SHOP'S PROPRIETOR.

After New York City, Chicago had one of the country's largest bohemias. Chicago's bohemian area in Towertown, near the Michigan Avenue water tower, contained the Wind Blew Inn (later possibly relocated to Greenwich Village), the Green Mask, and the Blue Mouse, among many others. Towertown tea rooms' brand of bohemianism was reputedly made up of run-down buildings, grime, candles, and nudes drawn on walls. In the 1920s local women organized "Seeing Bohemia" tours for 75¢ a person, and some places allegedly had themselves raided to draw "slummers" from outside the area. Like the Village, Towertown too became the victim of commercialization and rising real estate values, with its peak from 1912 to 1924. By the late 1920s business entrepreneurs were looking for profits in contrived "nutty" clubs, such as the Coal Scuttle and the Gold Coast House of Correction, driving any remaining bohemians deep into seclusion.

More durable, in Chicago, was the influence of Harriet (Tilden) Vaughn Moody's catering business, poetry salon, and tea rooms. Bohemian poets and actors were never so rewarded with good food as they were by Harriet. As a young schoolteacher driven by a desperate need for more income to support her mother, she had started catering out of her home on Groveland Avenue in the 1890s. Soon she was asked to supply Marshall Field and railroad dining cars with her products. During her brief marriage to poet William Vaughn Moody, who died in 1910, she became well-known as a benefactor of poets. Around 1912 she catered the tea room at the Little Theatre on the fourth floor of the Fine Arts Building on Michigan Avenue. Her successful Home Delicacies Association catering business, according to its stylish art deco brochure of 1928, proved that women's home cooking could "meet the most selective demands." Around the mid-1920s Harriet started Au Petit Gourmet at 615 North Michigan Avenue, then in 1927 began Au Grand Gourmet on Delaware

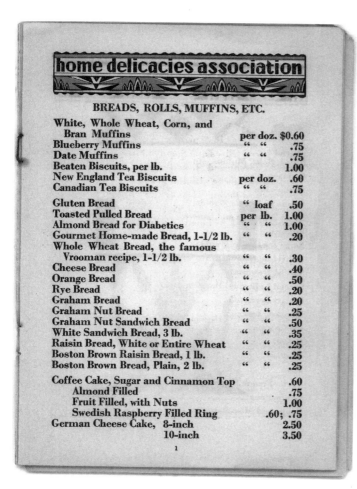

home delicacies association

BREADS, ROLLS, MUFFINS, ETC.

White, Whole Wheat, Corn, and Bran Muffins	per doz.	$0.60
Blueberry Muffins	" "	.75
Date Muffins	" "	.75
Beaten Biscuits, per lb.		1.00
New England Tea Biscuits	per doz.	.60
Canadian Tea Biscuits	" "	.75
Gluten Bread	" loaf	.50
Toasted Pulled Bread	per lb.	1.00
Almond Bread for Diabetics	" "	1.00
Gourmet Home-made Bread, 1-1/2 lb.	" "	.20
Whole Wheat Bread, the famous Vrooman recipe, 1-1/2 lb.	" "	.30
Cheese Bread	" "	.40
Orange Bread	" "	.50
Rye Bread	" "	.20
Graham Bread	" "	.20
Graham Nut Bread	" "	.25
Graham Nut Sandwich Bread	" "	.50
White Sandwich Bread, 3 lb.	" "	.35
Raisin Bread, White or Entire Wheat	" "	.25
Boston Brown Raisin Bread, 1 lb.	" "	.25
Boston Brown Bread, Plain, 2 lb.	" "	.25
Coffee Cake, Sugar and Cinnamon Top		.60
Almond Filled		.75
Fruit Filled, with Nuts		1.00
Swedish Raspberry Filled Ring		.60; .75
German Cheese Cake, 8-inch		2.50
10-inch		3.50

1

FRONT-COVER DECORATION AND A PAGE FROM THE CIRCA 1928 CATALOG OF THE HOME DELICACIES ASSOCIATION, FOUNDED BY HARRIET VAUGHN MOODY IN CHICAGO.

Place. On Sunday evening the tables were removed from the biggest room at Au Petit Gourmet and poets such as Robert Frost, Carl Sandburg, and Edna St. Vincent Millay read their works.

Beyond big cities, artists' colonies in small resort towns also nurtured bohemianism and tea rooms. Perkins Cove in Ogunquit, Maine, was an established artists' colony by the end of the 1800s and had several tea rooms in the early 1900s, among them the long-lived Whistling Oyster. Provincetown, the summer home of Greenwich Village thespians, had a tea room operated by a group of male art students. Costumed in sailor suits, they served tea and sandwiches at the Sixes and Sevens and sang and played musical instruments. The nighttime cover charge was set at 11¢ because the tea room closed at 11 P.M., when the last bus ran along Commercial Street.

❖ ❖ ❖

Largely due to their Greenwich Village fame, tea rooms became known for their relation to the arts. As the trade journal *The American Restaurant* observed in 1924, tea rooms were "associated with people who work in art and literature." Proprietors of small tea rooms, wherever they were located, felt some pressure to bow to the clamor for a bohemian atmosphere, even if (as critics said) it was achieved by "all sort of fantastic effects such as Oriental pottery, grotesque nick-nacks and other 'trick' embellishments." Whimsical tea room names, too, became almost expected thanks to the Village. Now, each and every tea room, if it was to prosper, had to possess unique charm. American women with the means to dine out were looking for something special and were not in the market for mass culture and standardized fare. The influence of Greenwich Village would be felt most strongly in urban tea rooms, but even roadside tea houses in the smallest towns in New England would aspire to be distinctive and atmospheric, with at least a hint of artistry.

CHAPTER THREE

Roadside Resorts

Until the automobile was graduated from the class of luxuries into that of necessities, tea-shops were successful only in the larger cities. Today they flourish in the smallest hamlets and flaunt their copper kettles and blue teapots on every broad highway.

—"AT THE SIGN OF THE TEA-ROOM," *GOOD HOUSEKEEPING*, JULY 1917

Around 1912, about the same time as the tea room craze was getting under way in Greenwich Village, tea houses were springing up along roadsides in rural areas where automobile traffic was becoming sufficiently heavy. There was money to be made catering to the motoring public, and women's magazines were quick to spread the word of the new opportunities. From farmers' wives and daughters to vacationing city schoolteachers, women eagerly responded to the possibilities, and tea rooms became established in the first wave of roadside eating places in America. Opening a tea room, said one woman in 1913, was the "answer to the modern girl's plaint: 'After college, what?'"

Women were attracted to the business because it was said to require little capital or experience. Charlene Baker, proprietor of Buttercup Hill in Lunenburg, Massachusetts, started with one kerosene stove and a room seating twelve "not very comfortably." Unlike others featured in magazines, she at least knew how to cook. She made cakes, pies, and mayonnaise at home each day and delivered it all in her car. Anne Sullivan, by contrast, freely professed in *American Cookery* that she had taken over management of a rural tea room one summer even though her cooking skills were minimal. "No grown woman could have been less well versed than I in housewifely arts," she admitted. She attributed her success to large portions and the ability to understand human psychology.

Grace Knudson, operator of the Torii Tea House in Castine, Maine, started her place "on a lark." She and a friend rented a warehouse basement along a pier for $5 to entertain friends in their very own private tea room. As "Dame Chance" would have it, Grace said, their party was interrupted by yachters wanting tea and asking to buy the Oriental fabrics she had used to adorn the bare room. Fifteen years later, her profitable tea room and Asian import business were being featured as an inspiration to other women in *Woman's Home Companion*.

In many of the magazine pieces, proprietors were young women who disliked their city jobs, feeling trapped by low salaries and mindless work. "We are merely parts of a monstrous machine," said two sisters in a 1911 *Ladies' Home Journal* story as they made plans to move back home and open a tea room in an uncle's barn. Norma Bamman, proprietor of Pinkie's Pantry in Plainfield, New Jersey, left her studio apartment in New York City to open a tea room on a busy road to Metuchen. Her roadside bakery stand in front of her home and tea room, decorated with black-and-white-painted shelves lined with pink oilcloth, was so attractive she won first prize in a nationwide Better Wayside Refreshment Stand contest sponsored by Mrs. John D. Rockefeller Jr. in 1928. Shocked at the rapid commercial devastation of the countryside, the judges commended Pinkie for preserving a beautiful, large tree near her stand. "Most roadside stand owners would have stupidly cut [it] down," they observed.

City schoolteachers who ran tea rooms during summer vacations often enjoyed success, in part because they understood the tastes and preferences of their affluent customers. The three Puffer sisters, two of whom were teachers in Brookline, Massachusetts, ran the Nobleboro Community Kitchen for three summers in the 1920s, serving a wealthy clientele en route to their summer places in Bar Harbor, Maine. One summer a former landlord attempted to run his own tea room in the same house they had rented the previous year, but he quickly met with failure despite having lured away one of their waitresses (along with some of their recipes she knew). In the words of Alice Puffer, "He underestimated the value of artistic appearance and failed to provide the awnings, umbrellas, and painted furniture which had made his

house attractive the year before." The Puffer sisters were proud of their style sense and that their customers recognized them as equals, with some patrons visiting them in their Brookline home or inviting them to the country club.

Not all roadside tea rooms were upscale, however. As driving became more commonplace and a more diverse motoring public took to the roads in the late 1920s, tea rooms accompanying roadside cabin camps, general stores, and gas stations opened. Often these were mom-and-pop operations, with mom running the tea room while pop pumped gas. Lacking the style and "class" of other roadside tea rooms, some of these tea rooms undoubtedly represented what highway beautification programs sought to eradicate. Cabin-camp and gas-station tea rooms were rarely depicted in women's magazines. Middle-class women who read *Ladies' Home Journal, Good Housekeeping,* or *House Beautiful* may have longed to have a tea room of their very own, but it is doubtful that their husbands wanted to exchange their business suits for greasy overalls.

More Cars, More Tea Rooms

The earliest rural tea rooms were located in resort areas such as Cape Cod, the White Mountains, and along Maine's seacoast. Examples include Kennebunkport, Maine's Periwinkle, which opened in 1907 (and was run by a Mount Holyoke College alumna) and Lake Sunapee's Cheshire Cat in

New Hampshire in 1908. However, real growth in the number of road-side tea rooms did not occur until car travel increased substantially in the teens. Passenger car registration jumped from a mere eight thousand in 1900 to nine hundred thousand in 1912, making a well-located rural retail business a practical possibility.

In the early days most tea rooms were in New England and the Northeast, where the number of automobile registrations was high and roads were better. In the teens, when car travel was still primarily recreational, touring parties tended to be large, with four to seven people in one vehicle. A few carloads could fill a small tea room. Tea rooms acknowledged their debt to the automobile with names like Motorists' Rest, the Sign of the Motor Car, Ontheway, and the Edgewood Inn's "Automobilists' Tea Room," in Greenwich, Connecticut, in 1913.

The opening of new roads, such as the Mohawk Trail in Massachusetts in October of 1914, spurred tea room development. By the 1920s the

"The Sign of the MotorCar" Dennis

scenic Mohawk Trail, which ran from Boston to Williamstown across the top of the state, was dotted with tea rooms. "Make a stop before going over the top" was the slogan of the Totem Tea Room, located near the road's highest point. Alice Brown started selling maple sugar hearts at her Sweetheart Tea Room on the Trail shortly after it was completed, advertising, "Stop for your sweetheart." Her small shop seated sixty, and she offered guests as many waffles as they could eat, demonstrating the generous hospitality people expected in rural areas. In other areas, picturesque highways, such as the mid-Atlantic Susquehanna Trail, New York's Albany Post Road, and the Boston Post Road paralleling Long Island Sound were also tea room venues.

Widely used automobile guidebooks of the early 1920s were filled with advertisements from Eastern tea rooms and small inns, most run by women. The number of advertisements graphically showed how rapidly these establishments had spread along the roadways. The Blue Books and Green Books, as they were known, furnished drivers with a kind of narrative map that pointed out landmarks and told them where to turn on the

TREE TOPS
STUDIO GIFT SHOP

GIFT SHOP & PIAZZA
TEA ROOM
Sign of the
Yellow Windmill
Bradford St. at the
end of Kendall Lane
PROVINCETOWN
Massachusetts

MILLER SISTERS' TEA HOUSE.
SOUTH MANCHESTER, CONN.
"FOOD of MARK"

The Lodge
Telephone, Amsterdam 1964-W
Tourists Accommodated

NOT A COUNTRY TEA ROOM
A City Tea Room in the Country
A STOPPING PLACE for FASTIDIOUS PEOPLE
EVERYTHING DAINTILY SERVED

On the Highway
One Mile East of
Amsterdam, N. Y.

THE GREEN KETTLE TEA ROOM
ALTON BAY, N. H.
Lunches. Special Mid-day Dinner.
Box Lunches put up for Motorists.
*Fancy hand-made Souvenirs. Tatted Handkerchiefs,
Ties, etc. Confectionery.*
Open from June 17th to Oct. 1st.   Frances I. Carroll, Prop.

Green Arbor Tea Room

Lexington Road
Concord, Mass.
Opens April 19

Lunch Afternoon Tea Supper
Limited Number Accommodated Overnight
Phone Concord 371 M

The **CORNER CUPBOARD TEA HOUSE** *Ascutneyville, Vt.*
Excellent luncheons—served on open porch. Antiques. Loom work. Exclusive gifts
OPEN MAY 1st.   Overnight Guests.   Telephone 4331   MISS NEWHALL'S

The White Tea House
Greenfield, Massachusetts
437 MAIN STREET   OPPOSITE POST OFFICE
LUNCHEON, AFTERNOON TEA, SUPPER
MOTOR INN—Phone 660—OVERNIGHT ACCOMMODATIONS

THE GREEN TEA CUP INN AND TEA HOUSE
NEWPORT   Herkimer County   NEW YORK
A convenient and attractive stopping place fourteen miles north of
Herkimer on road to Old Forge, Watertown and Adirondacks.
ACCOMMODATIONS OVERNIGHT   MRS. H. S. LOTTIMER   Tel. Newport 123

ADVERTISEMENTS FROM
AUTOMOBILE BLUE AND
GREEN BOOKS, 1921–24.

confusing, unmarked roads of that time. Tea room advertisers made the most of their convenient locations on improved state roads or "million-dollar highways," and their nearness to attractions such as Old Forge, Ausable Chasm, and the Adirondacks in New York. Travelers were advised to look for the "Blue Sign," the "Coat-of-Arms Sign," or the "Sign of the Yellow Windmill."

In the 1920s, tea rooms were commonplace in many parts of the country. However, few early roadside tea rooms were to be found in the rural Midwest, or in the West except along the Pacific coast. Only a small number of tea rooms existed in the South (where eating out became commonplace only after the Second World War) except along the coastal route to Florida, which was heavily traveled by Easterners. But in areas where they flourished, major roads were overcrowded with tea rooms by the late 1920s. In 1924, according to tea room columnist and consultant Ralph Elliott, "Competition in some localities, and especially along the more heavily travelled motor roads, is so keen that it makes adequate returns almost impossible." Two English tourists traveling by car in 1928 were amazed at the number of signs for inns and tea rooms they saw along the roadside in Connecticut, most offering chicken dinners for one dollar.

Gentrifying the Countryside

Since most patrons were city dwellers, a roadside tea room was most likely to thrive if it was located within easy driving distance of a big city. This was true of the small tea room that helped build the Knott's Berry

Farm complex of tourist attractions in 1927. At that time, twenty-two miles from downtown Los Angeles was just about the right distance for a Sunday drive. The Bird of Paradise Tea Room, specializing in Kadota fig products, in California's San Fernando Valley, was another possible destination. The Tumble Down Tea House prospered because of its location not far north of Washington, D.C. New York City, of course, supported the largest number of outlying rural tea rooms. One of these, the Rainbow Tea House in Pound Ridge, New York, designed an eye-catching card that explained that New Yorkers should take the White Plains–Bronx River Parkway for forty-three miles and told them which roads were paved and where they could get gasoline too. Some tea rooms spent fall, winter, and spring in the city, following their clientele to the country for the summer. In summer of 1928 the House by the Side of the Road was opposite the Hunt Club, near Brown Deer on the Green Bay Road, while its "town studio" did business in Milwaukee the rest of the year. Smaller cities too could provide customers for a roadside tea room. The Headley Inn and Tea Room operated five miles west of Zanesville, Ohio, in 1925.

Motoring city-dwellers wanted to find a quaint, old-fashioned past when they visited rural areas—but theirs was an idealized notion of rural America that was often at odds with reality. Rural landscapes that had been commercialized often disappointed them, while the locals' attitudes and customs—which actually were old-fashioned—annoyed them. They viewed the countryside esthetically, looking for beautiful vistas and picturesque farms, while the rural folks saw it pragmatically. If a tree was in the way, the farmer had no qualms about cutting it down. If a dollar was to be made, he installed a gas pump in his front yard or erected shantylike cabins. City dwellers wanted to dispense with formality and return to the simple life. They wanted to relax and be comfortable while out for a drive; men preferred not to wear coats and ties. Touring parties wanted quick, unfussy meals. But small-town hotels often expected guests to dress properly for meals and to spend time at the table waiting for their five courses to arrive. Tourists of the motorcar age grew tired of the stuffiness of old nineteenth-century-style resorts, with their Victorian interiors furnished with plush furniture, dusty carpets, and stuffed animals in glass domes. They disapproved of small-town roadhouses, where heavy drinking went on. Women traveling alone expected to be served without discrimination. All in all, city dwellers wanted to enjoy the countryside on their own terms.

During earlier decades when the railroad was the dominant form of transportation, vacationers had spent their summers at huge resort hotels. Like cruise ships, these resorts were worlds unto themselves, offering guests days packed with scheduled activities and punctuated by long hours in the dining room. The advent of the automobile, as Warren Belasco has shown in *Americans on the Road*, led people to reject resort hotels, opting instead for the freedom to explore the countryside at their own pace, stopping whenever they felt like it.

THE PROPRIETOR OF POLLY'S TRAVELED TO EUROPE TO ACQUIRE DECORATIVE ITEMS FOR HER EARLY-1920S TEA ROOM IN COLEBROOK, NEW HAMPSHIRE.

TEA AT THE BLUE LANTERN INN

Small inns and tea rooms, often operated together, were the beneficiaries of the new style of travel and proved adept at fulfilling city dwellers' expectations of the countryside. According to a 1916 story in the magazine *Country Life in America*, most motorists preferred a simple lunch of sandwiches and tea served under a tree "to a much more pretentious meal in some hotel—even a good one." Polly's Place, in New Hampshire, specifically derived its patronage from guests of the nearby White Mountain hotels who were seeking a "radical change from hotel food." Around 1922, the Ragged Robin Tea Shop, also in the White Mountains, catered to people in a hurry, recognizing, its owner said, that "the tourist of to-day, who rushes through the country at top speed, is not looking for a big hotel where he may leisurely eat a course dinner." Although tea rooms were billed as places of rest and relaxation, they also served as the gentry's version of a fast-food restaurant.

Car travelers not only wanted their food quick, they also wanted it at all hours. Many roadside tea rooms accommodated travelers who arrived late or at odd times. According to the owner of the Ragged Robin, she was "prepared to serve them at a moment's notice." The Brookside Tea House in Manomet, Massachusetts, was typical in requiring reservations for dinner but providing tea and sandwiches at all hours. Such flexibility was quite a departure from hotels' fixed and rigid meal schedules.

Motorists loved the quaintness of the countryside, but their affection for bygone times did not include commonplace old roadhouses and saloons. "Quieter folks of good taste," as a *Good Housekeeping* story characterized tea room patrons, regarded roadhouses as low class and disreputable. Although roadhouses were the true successors to Colonial inns (where drinking was heavy indeed), the magazine's 1911 "Taverns and Tea

Rooms as a Business for Women" preferred to give tea rooms this ancestral heritage. The story found a parallel between the contemporary American tea room, the English inn, the French auberge, and the American inn of the Revolutionary era, conveniently forgetting the alcoholic heritage these forerunners shared. A man who took over a location previously occupied by a notorious roadhouse in 1916 found to his dismay that he could not get any customers for his tea room, the Huckleberry Inn. The only people who entered his door were looking for alcoholic refreshments. He visited every minister in the seven adjacent towns and told them he "was removing a canker sore from the public highway." They remained unconvinced until he hosted free Sunday-school picnics at his tea room. Once he proved himself, anti-alcohol sentiment worked in his favor and he gained patronage. By 1919 a restaurant-industry trade journal observed that rural tea shops, the majority owned by women, were successfully competing against roadhouses. The coming of national Prohibition the following year would bolster their success.

Chicken and Waffles

City dwellers dreamed of the fresh produce and honest cookery they would find in the country, but were horrified at the dismal meals they actually encountered in small-town hotels and eateries. On a road trip in 1915 Emily Post recorded that her hotel dinner featured "greasy fried fish, cold bluish potatoes, [and] sliced raw onions," all tasting as though they "had come out of the same dishwater." A New York City party of weekend tourists endured a similar fate. Longing for fresh strawberries,

they were served instead a meal of sour bread, slate-colored coffee, tough steak, and prunes. Wise tea room proprietors, by contrast, were prepared to supply the fresh food their customers expected. A Vermont proprietor said in 1923 that she had built her reputation over the past ten years simply by providing "plenty of fresh butter and cream." Like many, she specialized in fried-chicken dinners and creamed chicken on toast. Chicken and waffles was an ubiquitous item on roadside tea room menus, so much so that by the late 1920s some travelers were weary of it. "Thank God for a place that doesn't offer chicken and waffles," a well-traveled customer told a Connecticut tea room owner in 1928. But most city dwellers liked this dish, and the tradition of eating a chicken dinner in the country would prevail for some time. It would be years before changes in the chicken-raising industry would make chicken cheap and plentiful in city supermarkets.

Tea rooms specialized in preparing a few simple dishes well. Believing, she said, that her guests found long hotel menus "as tedious to read as a Theodore Dreiser novel," Cecil Reams, proprietor of Long Ridge,

Connecticut's Wayside Tea Room, kept hers short, as did most tea rooms. The college student who ran the Rest-a-bit Inn offered only her "Rest-a-bit spread," which consisted of tea or lemonade, ham, tongue, tea cakes, bread and butter, olives, potato salad, and home-made preserves. She thought her $1 charge was "extortionate" (the equivalent of about $15 now), but patrons didn't seem to mind. At the Sign of the Motor Car on Cape Cod, the original menu was for afternoon tea only and consisted solely of four kinds of tea, toast, one kind of sandwich (lettuce), three kinds of cake, and ice cream. The Green Arbor Tea House in Concord, Massachusetts, in 1917 had only two kinds of sandwiches, lettuce and olive, in addition to cheese dreams and "mystery cake."

The slogan of Cecil Reams's Wayside Tea Room, "For the luxury-jaded," revealed her keen understanding of the city dweller's wish for simple food. In New England, tea rooms often featured homely items such as cinnamon toast, doughnuts, and Saturday-night specials of brown bread and baked beans. The Yellow Cat in South Wallingford, Vermont, specialized in maple products. A featured dinner was waffles with creamed chicken, followed by waffles with maple syrup. Experts advised roadside tea room operators to keep the homemade taste in their food by emphasizing "the quality of their ingredients" rather than "the elaborateness of their decoration." Meringues and fluted frostings were best left to the professional bakers, they said.

Although it was good if tea rooms could grow their own food, said experts, it was not necessarily economical. By the late 1920s it was cheaper to buy fruit and vegetables from truck farms. Also, aside from eggs, dairy products could not easily be obtained in the country, instructed a 1932 correspondence course. Nevertheless, many tea rooms did grow their own food or obtain it locally. In the late 1920s the Puffer sisters got their chickens from their Maine neighbors and picked peas from their uncle's garden. The Lone Pine Inn in the Midwest had three cows and churned its own butter. Polly gathered eggs from her own hens, while the Lilacs, in South Hadley, Massachusetts, grew New England favorites, strawberries and asparagus.

Just Like Home, but Without Electricity

While it was desirable to have a tea house that looked quaint, roadside proprietors yearned for modern conveniences, particularly in the kitchen. Absolutely no one would have argued with the opinion expressed in *Woman's Home Companion:* "Too much cannot be said in favor of electricity for tea room use." Many roadside places had no electricity or running water. In the early 1920s only the lucky few had a gas range or a magical refrigerator "which makes ice cubes of just the right size." The alternative was to break up large chunks of block ice with an ice bag and a mallet. And this they did, because iced tea was a popular summer beverage. It was common to do all the cooking on a three-burner oil stove. The Tumble-Down Tea Room near Washington, D.C., turned out chicken dinners with lima beans and corn on one, and the Puffers' Nobleboro Community Kitchen managed just fine with theirs. The three Puffer sisters had a harder time, though, the summer they rented a house without running water. The proprietors' brother wore himself out making twenty-five hundred trips carrying water in buckets from a well a block away. Also lacking electricity that summer, they cooked at night with oil lamps while

WENHAM TEA HOUSE, WENHAM, MASS. 6.

THE WENHAM TEA HOUSE WAS BE-
GUN IN 1912 BY THE WENHAM VIL-
LAGE IMPROVEMENT SOCIETY, IN
MASSACHUSETTS. THE HOUSE SHOWN
HERE WAS BUILT IN 1916, AND THE
TEA KETTLE AND TABBY CAT SIGN
HUNG FROM THE CORNER OF THE
HOUSE. PHOTOS OF GUESTS AND
KITCHEN CIRCA 1920.

diners ate by candlelight. Many roadside tea rooms were open only during the warm months, but the owner of the Shaker Inn in Shakertown, Kentucky, was pleased when a new heating system enabled her to stay open year-round in 1940.

The absence of conveniences did not faze the customers, whose attentions were turned elsewhere. They were more interested in good food, a pleasant location, and homelike surroundings untainted by a "grasping and commercial atmosphere." Roadside tea rooms were advised to avoid cash registers, or cigar and candy cases, which looked too mercenary, and to keep their eating places small. Consultant Ralph Elliott said that to provide a homelike feeling a roadside tea room should seat about seventy persons. Home atmosphere was also conveyed by the hostess, often the owner or her partner, who provided the all-important "personal touch." Charleen Baker of the Buttercup Hill Tea Room pledged in writing to her guests that she would abide by "home quality." Many tea rooms, such as the White Rabbit in Buzzards Bay, Massachusetts, also served second helpings at no additional charge. Others gave away free apples, maple sugar candies, or bags of cookies for children so as not to send the dangerous message "We want nothing from you but your money." It was assumed, though not always true, that a woman's personal touch would guarantee cleanliness and scrupulous food preparation. Indeed, the highest praise a customer could give a restaurant in the 1920s was attained by a tea room owner in Bangor, Maine, when a patron told her, "I'm not afraid to eat hash here."

Country Charm

Being homelike, though, was not enough to get speeding cars to stop. A successful roadside tea room had to project enough quaintness to passing motorists to draw them in. It needed curb appeal, and lots of it. The house had to be distinctive and charming, something out of the ordinary. A beautiful natural setting was helpful and so were attractive signboards and an appealing name.

The perfect roadside tea house, according to Ralph Elliott in 1926, would be found in an old-fashioned, rambling storybook house, which beckoned the visitor from room to room. It would be furnished with hand-loomed rugs, calico curtains, and "tables of time-worn antiquity." Outdoors, the house would be sheltered by elms, "while a silvery brook tinkles its way though the old-fashioned garden behind." A remarkable number of roadside tea rooms fit these characteristics. Hand-hooked rugs, simple antique furniture, and homemade curtains were almost standard in successful tea rooms. Tea house architecture ranged from old Georgian saltboxes to shake-covered Cape Cod–style houses. Outside New England, bungalows and stucco cottages reminiscent of the English Cotswolds were common homes to tea rooms.

Simplicity in decor did not necessarily mean rusticity (although the cabin look was a popular favorite). The Gray Parrot Inn and Tea Room in Deerfield, Massachusetts, touted its "artistic appointments." It was not unknown for roadside proprietors to hire an architect or interior decorator to help remodel their tea room. The Lone Pine Inn's decorator chose light gray for interior walls, accented by woodwork mottled with blue-green. A wild-looking cretonne fabric with orange-red tree trunks and blue-green leaves on a black background provided the curtains. The material had been sold at a markdown, apparently because it was too daring for the area. The tea room proprietor wondered if she'd gone too far with this fabric, but when she went back to the store for more, she discovered her tea room had made it so popular it had sold out.

Natural beauty was important for the roadside tea room. In summer, before air-conditioning, trees and shade were appealing to overheated motorists. Edna Ferguson's Shady Nook in Cataumet, Massachusetts, promised a cooling respite, as did the Elm Shade in Great Barrington, Massachusetts. Often tea room guests ate on terraces, verandas, or piazzas—as yards, porches, and patios were romantically known then. Tea rooms made outdoor dining popular at a time when it was uncommon, capitalizing on the affluent classes' interest in "getting back to nature." Guests often wandered around tea house grounds or lingered in the garden. The Lilacs provided their patrons with butterfly nets. If a tea room was lucky enough to have spectacular scenery, they made much of it in their advertising. The Yacht Club Tea House in Newport, Vermont, boasted in the 1924 automobile Blue Book that it had "magnificent scenery," while the Iron Kettle in Waverly, New York, exclaimed about the beautiful Chemung Valley, which it overlooked.

The names and signboards of roadside tea rooms were often modeled on Colonial taverns, with words like *green, blue, bird, old, tavern, mill, maple,*

A FINE SIGNBOARD AT THE CAT & BAGPIPES, LOCATION UNKNOWN. MAPLE SYRUP GIFTS WERE COMMONLY SOLD IN NEW ENGLAND TEA ROOMS.

pine, inn, and *wayside* predominating. Roadside tea room names became so well-known as a "genre" that in the mid-1930s when the trade journal *Restaurant Management* provided readers with reproducible logos they could use, a third of them bore common tea room names such as the Blue Bird, the Green Shutter, and the Lantern. Popular signboards often featured birds, animals, or teapots. Around 1916, famed illustrator Maxfield Parrish designed a sign for friends who owned the Tea Tray in Cornish, New Hampshire, depicting an eighteenth-century couple relaxing at a tea table. The couple-at-a-table design motif would also prove perennially popular for signs and menu covers.

Box Lunches and Sleeping Porches

It was a rare roadside tea room that did not also have a sideline business, which could range from selling gifts or antiques to renting rooms to operating a gas station. Given the seasonal nature of the roadside business, tea rooms had to make the most of their earning potential. Those that started out just offering afternoon tea soon discovered they had to add meals and other revenue-producers if they were to survive. Overnight accommodations and gift shops were by far the most popular sidelines. Food gifts were a natural extension, as were box lunches for automobile parties. Some, like the Betsey Buttles Tea House in Middlebury, Vermont, tried to cover all the bases. Its owners, Mrs. Griffen and Miss Buttles, claimed they had good coffee and a place that was "just a little different."

ETHEL FARLEY'S INN, TEA ROOM, AND GIFT SHOP IN FARLEY, MASSACHUSETTS.

TOP: VIEW FROM THE PORCH. BOTTOM: THE STAFF TAKES A BREAK.

They promised, "We can keep you overnight. We can give you a basket lunch."

Motor inn was the name adopted by many roadside businesses that offered tea, meals, and rooms. According to Helen Woods, who directed a tea room training school in the early 1920s, she coined this term to avoid

THE TEA CHEST, LOCATED ON THE MAIN HIGHWAY IN COCONUT GROVE, OPENED ON DECEMBER 22, 1921. *(Historical Association of Southern Florida)*

TWO SEASONS AT THE TEA CHEST

In warm climates the season for tourists and tea rooms ran from late fall through spring. The Tea Chest in Coconut Grove, Florida, was in business for just two seasons in 1922 and 1923, making a small profit for its two young owners, Patty Munroe and Alice Ayars. Patty was the daughter of Coconut Grove founder Ralph Munroe, who eliminated the letter *a* from Cocoanut in the village's name because he thought it confusing.

As was true of many tea rooms, business at the Tea Chest fluctuated drastically from day to day and week to week. A poor day could bring as few as two guests; a good day, dozens. Guests came from nearby Miami and other Florida towns, but with permanent addresses in New York, Pittsburgh, Chicago, Cleveland, Boston, and other cities mostly in the North. The proprietors were thrilled when they had a full house, "celebrated" guests (such as Mabel Loomis Todd or Mr. and Mrs. Cornelius Vanderbilt Jr.), and an empty larder by day's end. On a poor day, they consoled themselves with thoughts of the "pretty kimono cloth" on their tables and the presence of "only one baby cockroach."

A gift shop was a significant part of the Tea Chest, which served no meals, only afternoon tea. The shop ordered merchandise from all over the country, and even from abroad. Among their wares were copper items from the Friar Tuck Company in New York, chairs made by the Shakers of Mount Lebanon, New York ($3 apiece, including crating), Chinese imports from the Lantern Shop in Pittsfield, Massachusetts, and umbrellas from Yokohama, Japan. Harriet Sammons of Farmington, New Mexico, supplied them with Navajo blankets and jewelry, and they acquired bowls, vases, and candlesticks from the Cowan Pottery Studios of Rocky River, Ohio. Like all good tea room proprietors, Patty and Alice bent over backward to please guests, once shipping a coconut to a man in DeForest, Wisconsin. He wrote them a thank-you note saying it was "quite a curiosity" to the folks back home.

"dainty-sounding titles" (i.e., ones that would drive away men). It was used by the Little Brown House in Newtown, Connecticut, in 1925, and by the Motor Inn and French Tea Room in Milford, Pennsylvania. In April 1923, Anna Talmadge, proprietor of the Green Apple Inn in Keeseville, New York, wrote to Helen Woods, thanking her for the course and saying, "I am going ahead with great confidence and enlarging my Tea Room into a Motor Inn with fourteen rooms." More common than motor inns were tea rooms operated in the owner's house, with just one or two rooms reserved for overnight guests. Some inns and guest homes, particularly those in northern New England, supplemented their rooms with open-air sleeping porches, evidently an attraction in the 1920s. Tea rooms associated with cabin camps were found all over the United States by the 1930s and were the predecessors to motel coffee shops of later decades.

Food gifts covered the spectrum, from the Sweetheart's maple sugar hearts to native fruit, chicken soup, and cottage cheese, all of which were available at the Nobscot Mountain Tea House in South Sudbury, Massachusetts. Homemade pies, candies, roasted chickens, and preserves were widely sold too. Some tea rooms had less common food gifts. The tiny Log Cabin Tea Room in Denmark, Maine, specialized in homemade marshmallows, while the Snap Dragon in Kennebunk sold guava jelly from Florida. The Old Hundred in Southbury, Connecticut, had a range of offerings including homemade relishes, jams, and candies as well as fresh eggs. Proprietor Nellie Brown also sold salad bowls and birdhouses. Basket lunches were provided by the Nobscot Mountain Tea House and many others and were a delicious alternative to lunch at the ubiquitous hot dog stand.

Handcrafted articles were the most popular kind of nonfood gift sold at roadside tea rooms. These could be hand-sewn or embroidered items, woven scarves and mats, or rugs. Polly's specialized in peasant pottery and all kinds of items with a parrot motif. Handicrafts by Native Americans such as baskets, weavings, pottery, and beadwork were also in great demand in the 1920s. The Green Arbor Tea House in Concord, Massachusetts, sold hand-crocheted "doylies" from the Cape. Gifts made from local materials included balsam pillows in New Hampshire, and magnolia products at the Blue Gables Tea Shoppe in the Arkansas Ozarks. Gifts served as both decorations and revenue producers, and any kind of connection with their makers also added a dimension of interest. As someone commented, "The bare walls of frame or adobe tea houses need no other ornament than the Navaho blankets, beaded moccasins, bags or necklaces and exquisitely fashioned baskets of the native Indian. Sales are increased by the presence of even one *real Indian*."

Often a roadside tea room's gift shop was run to raise funds for impoverished communities of craftspeople who made the items for sale. Polly's Place sold handmade Colonial bedspreads and table covers for the benefit of the Southern Industrial Association. In Connecticut, the Dog Team Tea House was operated by the Grenfell Labrador Industries and sold hooked rugs made by that renowned organization. The Val-Kill Tea Room in Dutchess County, New York, was run in conjunction with a rural crafts economic development project.

As obvious a combination as roadside tea rooms and gas stations might have seemed, only a few managed to project an attractive appearance or the right ambience. Aunt Em's Tea Room in Derry, New Hampshire, went awry in a 1921 Green Book advertisement, offering "smokes" and misspelling sherbet. The Light House Service Station and Tea Room in Henryville, Pennsylvania, was one of the more successful. It presented travelers with a spick-and-span stucco roadside service stopover, far from the ocean, but with cool-looking green-and-red-striped awnings. Walker's Jack O'Lantern Log Cabin Tea Room and Service Station on Route

HUMBLE-LOOKING WHITCOMB'S TEA ROOM IN NORTH HATFIELD, MASSACHUSETTS, SOLD SINCLAIR GASOLINE AND ICE CREAM.

9W, two miles south of Kingston, New York, had a rough-looking exterior but a surprisingly attractive interior. Furnished with Windsor chairs, it had jack-o'-lanterns stenciled on the curtains and on the shades of the lamps that sat at the end of each table.

❖ ❖ ❖

Despite the occasional criticism that roadside tea rooms were amateurish or were gift shops disguised as eating places, they succeeded in winning over a good percentage of travelers and Sunday drivers in the days before chain restaurants. Duncan Hines, whose guide to roadside eateries, *Adventures in Good Eating*, came out in the 1930s, was a staunch fan, awarding tea rooms about a quarter of his seals of approval. Even an eminent food critic like M.F.K. Fisher admitted in 1950 that when she traveled in unpromising locales, she found the regional cooking in "tearoomy" places usually made them the best bet. Although many dropped *tea room* from their names and some eventually added cocktails to their menus, a number of roadside tea rooms begun in the 1920s or before survived well into the 1950s.

CHAPTER FOUR

Ye Olde Tea Shoppe

The house itself must be quaint, or picturesque, or distinctive in some way, so that the eye is arrested and the passerby is made anxious to investigate further.

—*TEA-ROOM MANAGEMENT*, AUGUST 1922

America's love affair with quaintness, which sparred so persistently with modernism throughout the twentieth century, colored the development of tea rooms in many ways. Most tea room owners seemed to prefer the old to the new. Some linked their enterprises to the past, as though they were direct descendants of

Colonial innkeepers. Many chose old buildings for their businesses and capitalized on their antique qualities rather than modernizing them. Financial necessity sometimes played a role, since barns, mills, sheds, blacksmith shops, and stables could usually be rented for less than conventional retail locations. Low rent was important to tea room operators—who were commonly refused business loans—but unusual locations were viewed as more than merely economical. Often the sheer strangeness and novelty of a building recommended it for a tea shop and helped to attract curious patrons who sought escape from modern standardization, ceaselessly looking for "something different."

In the early twentieth century the styles and sentiments of the Victorian period held few charms. Given the interest in Victorian-themed tea rooms today, it is worth noting how unpopular that era was with proprietors and their patrons during the tea room's full flourish. Then, Victorian decor was considered ugly and out-of-date. It was "history," but in the negative sense. The Lewis Tea Room Training Course, a 1920s correspondence course, urged prospective owners to avoid the dreary, cluttered interiors of the previous generation, which it said typically had walls painted red, green, or "muddy" brown or covered with large-patterned wallpapers and a "hodgepodge" of pictures in gilt or golden oak frames. It also advised against the elaborate Wilton or Persian carpets popular with Victorians, "heavy stuffed furniture of faded plush," and windows swathed in brocade and tied with cords and tassels. The overall effect, bluntly asserted the lesson on decor, resembled "a well draped hearse." Although it was much older, Colo-

YELLOW LANTERN TEA HOUSE
CONCORD *Mass.*
TELEPHONE 231 R

nial decor, in contrast to the Victorian, appeared fresher, more contemporary, even youthful.

Colonially Quaint, yet Up-to-Date

Although all kinds of novelty themes and names were associated with tea rooms, Colonial associations were by far the most prevalent. In part this can be explained by the number of tea rooms occupying antique houses in New England towns and countryside during the 1910s and 1920s, but this is not the whole story. Colonial motifs were to be found in other regions of the country too, and even in unexpected, countercultural places such as bohemian Greenwich Village. Colonial themes seemed especially effective in linking people to the past while propelling them into the future, and this held true especially for the Anglo-American strata who patronized tea rooms.

Ever since the Centennial Exposition in Philadelphia in 1876, interest in the country's early history had been keen, especially among Anglo-Americans. Antique collecting became popular in the late nineteenth century, and the Colonial Revival movement also exerted a strong influence on architecture and interior design. Women were prominent in the Colonial Revival, helping to preserve historic buildings, writing books on home life in Colonial days, forming sewing circles, and taking up Colonial crafts. The spinning wheel took on special meaning and came to epitomize the best of American womanhood's past. Many women saw it as a symbol of bygone female productivity in the days before household goods were produced in factories and middle-class women lived lives of idle femininity. Spinning wheels were often placed in front of tea room hearths, as though to imply that the proprietor had reclaimed a lost household function, not as spinner but in an analogous role as provider of food and hospitality.

In August of 1922, *Tea Room Management* ran a story that purportedly documented the idea that tea rooms were reincarnations of the Colonial past. It proclaimed the King's Arms, established in 1753, as New York's "first tea room." Its proprietor, Elizabeth Steele, succeeded in her venture, the magazine said, because she gave her masculine patrons the same kind of food they were accustomed to eating at home. Instead of the heavy meals usually found in taverns, she served tea and "home-made delicacies"

such as ham, chicken, "dainty salads, rich preserves, fine pastries and delicate cakes." The story's author, Mary C. Pickett, also claimed that early tea rooms like the King's Arms had been effaced by the "abnormal growth of business" in the middle of the nineteenth century. "It remained," she said, "for the 20th century to dig them from beneath the dust and rubbish of a century." Stories like this communicated to middle-class women that running a tea room was a noble continuation of ancestral activity, and quite compatible with the values of Anglo-American womanhood. The story also revealed the mildly subversive wish of supporters of the Colonial Revival movement to undermine the materialistic society brought about by the Industrial Revolution.

The arrival of the automobile, which so benefited roadside tea rooms, intensified interest in Colonial ways. Its ability to go anywhere, anytime,

challenged the track- and schedule-bound train, trol-
ley, and streetcar—modes of transportation that were
regarded as regimented and soulless. Although tech-
nologically modern, the automobile was seen as the
contemporary equivalent of horse-drawn transportation in olden days, and early advertisements invariably
played up this theme. Early motorists exploring unpaved rural roadways lined with old houses liked to
imagine that they had actually returned to the past—if
only to bring back a trophy rocking chair! Roadside
tea room owners responded by selling antiques and

by likening their tea rooms or tourist homes to Colonial inns. Their own
fascination with early America complemented the automobile owner's
notion that his or her vehicle was a latter-day stagecoach. Roadside tea
rooms often used coaching motifs on signs and adopted names reminiscent of those days.

Despite its old-fashioned allure, however, the Colonial Revival represented modernity in disguise. The automobile would rework the fiber of
everyday life in ways the stagecoach and the horse and buggy had not.
Colonial design also proved remarkably congruent with modern needs.
The spareness and clean surfaces of Colonial styles seemed more hygienic
than Victorian clutter, and indeed, new scientific discoveries were showing
that environmental pathogens caused disease. The elimination of carpet-
ing, heavy draperies, and plush furniture was regarded as a healthful
choice. Interior decor influenced by both the Arts & Crafts and the Colonial Revival movements featured wooden or wicker furniture, bare floors,
tables without tablecloths, and lightly curtained windows. As the Lewis Tea
Room Training Institute observed in its correspondence-course material
in 1923, Colonial-styled gateleg tables and Windsor chairs were a "most

happy choice." Windsor chairs, they stated, were "artistic, light, sanitary, and fit in anywhere." Thousands of proprietors adopted Windsor-style furnishings, making them the first choice in rural and city tea rooms alike.

Modeling behavior on life in Colonial times—whether imagined or real—provided a graceful transition into modernism. It helped women find a way to engage more fully in commerce while retaining their dignity and a connection to their American heritage. Identifying with a Colonial lifestyle that they believed was uninhibited and free of artificiality, they felt empowered to reject etiquette-bound Victorian conduct. Colonial style was interpreted as informal and unpretentious, inviting its users to act likewise. New York City's Tally-Ho Tea Room in an old stable of the Astor estate on East Thirty-fourth Street played successfully upon this notion. People accustomed to the "pomp" of hotels could eat there, said a 1923 magazine article, and get good food in "free and unrestrained surroundings."

In Greenwich Village, where spontaneity and informality ruled, quite

ONCE THE ASTOR STABLES, THE TALLY-HO WAS REINCARNATED AS A POPULAR HAUNT FOR THOSE LOOKING FOR THE QUAINT AND OFFBEAT.

TELEPHONE MURRAY HILL 5924

The Tally-Ho

LUNCHEON, AFTERNOON TEA AND DINNER 20 EAST 34th STREET, NEW YORK

a few tea rooms decorated their interiors with Colonial furnishings. In harmony with the Crumperie's rag rugs and parson's benches, Alice Mc-Collister's arranged cozy seating in high-backed settles. A mantel was decorated with pewter jugs and plates. Fireplaces with cozy inglenooks, which were common in Village tea shops, as well as candles and hand-crafted wares, harked back to an idyllic preindustrial past. The Village's futurist color schemes and "pagan" lifestyles somehow easily coexisted with nostalgia for things Colonial, suggesting that the future could be reconciled with the values of the past.

The Colonial Revival movement, as embodied in tea rooms, also seemed to promise that modern discontent could be offset by a return to tight-knit communities. Tea rooms presented themselves as centers of social life, alternatives to the urban anonymity of industrialized society. In Greenwich Village, where tea shop patrons lingered for hours playing chess or reading books, it was considered wonderful (and remarkable) that anyone could freely strike up a conversation with strangers at nearby tables. At least one 1920s newcomer to the Village made a fast bunch of friends when she invited everyone in the small tea room where she had eaten dinner to her apartment for an impromptu party.

Tea rooms upheld community in a number of ways. Urban and rural tea rooms were commonly used for club meetings and get-togethers. In Salem, Massachusetts, in 1917, a group of women met every week at the Puritan Tea House, and their husbands joined them there later for dinner. Other tea rooms, such as the Brown Owl in Marblehead, Massachusetts, offered special lunches for children whose mothers were away for the day. At a time when children were not welcome in many restaurants, a tea room in Richmond, Virginia, expressly designed their menu around nutritious meals that children loved, while others catered special-occasion children's tea parties. Tea rooms created the hostess role, a less intimidating female rendition of the maître d'. The hostess was responsible for creating a feeling of welcome and ease among guests. In the words of restaurant consultant Ralph Elliott, the hostess was "the mother, the nurse, the friend and the sweetheart" of the tea room, and critical to its ability to make guests feel at home.

Historic Houses, Inns, and Taverns

Automobile travel awakened interest in old buildings that had languished along little-used roads during the dominance of the railroad. Inns that had fallen into disuse when the railroad had come were now refurbished and reopened to serve motorists. Tea room proprietors "hunted out and leased...houses of Revolutionary or earlier period," approvingly noted Elise Lathrop in her 1926 book, *Early American Inns and Taverns*. The Windsor Historical Society operated the Betsy Kob Tea-Room and museum in Connecticut. The 1640 Burnham House in Ipswich, Massachusetts, was restored and operated as an inn and tea room in 1920, and the Bottle Hill Tea Shop, in Madison, New Jersey, was located in the barroom of a Revolutionary inn. Although most historic houses and inns were in the Northeast, there were exceptions. The Georgian Tea Room was established in 1929 in the Old Pink House of 1771 in Savannah, Georgia, while the old Walker Tavern, erected in 1832, became a tea room and antique shop in Brooklyn, Michigan.

Many tea rooms were located in historic houses, some operated to raise funds for restoring the structure or an associated nonprofit venture. The Winslow House in Marshfield, Massachusetts, supported itself this

way, while the Shed Tea-House in Salem raised money for the House of Seven Gables Settlement. The Society for the Preservation of New England Antiquities operated the Blue Anchor Tea House in the 1670 Swett-Ilsley House in Newbury, Massachusetts. The Connecticut Society of Colonial Dames ran a tea room in the old taproom of Buell's Marlborough Inn, a tavern from the Revolutionary period. Tea-drinking patrons undoubtedly chuckled at the story of the hill outside the barroom door from which inebriated patrons of bygone days were said to have rolled downward toward home. The Dames also operated a tea room in the historic Webb House in Wethersfield from 1919 to 1924. Not successful as a money raiser, its biggest season's profit came to $8.

Historic-house tea room proprietors often took inspiration, and sometimes their business name, from a renowned figure of history who once lived there. The 1923 "Tea Room Booklet," published by *Woman's Home Companion*, recommended that tea room proprietors search for "some quaint old character of the past associated with your village or the house itself." Publicizing the historic character, the booklet said, would "let him do some free advertising for you." Sometimes the historic character was a man, but as often as not women tea room proprietors touted a female from the past. A mother and daughter in Connecticut were inspired to name their 1918 tea room after their ancestor Prudence Seymour, while Ye

THE PRUDENCE SEYMOUR TEA ROOM AND GIFT SHOP WAS LOCATED FOUR MILES NORTH OF NEW MILFORD, ON THE ROAD BETWEEN DANBURY AND LITCHFIELD, CONNECTICUT.

Bradford Arms in Plymouth, Massachusetts, proclaimed itself the former home of Tabitha Plaskett, the first woman schoolteacher. Others associated themselves with male figures too famous to ignore, such as the Hermitage Tea Room in Hohokus, New Jersey, which reminded patrons that they were visiting the house where Aaron Burr was married. The Webster Place in Franklin, New Hampshire, was the former home of Daniel Webster and had once been an old schoolhouse. Guests were served lunch or tea on "original" old school desks. The Old Homestead Tea Room and Inn in Cornwall, New York, boasted that it was where George Washington had received news of the battle of Stony Point, and the Latham Tea Room in Lincoln, Illinois, claimed it had once had frequent visits from Abraham Lincoln.

Tea room owners were delighted when they acquired an old building that still had an unspoiled interior, especially if it had survived from the Colonial period. In 1918, as an architect restored the Greenley Tea Garden in Greenwich, Connecticut, he made a lucky discovery of an old fireplace in the kitchen that had been boarded up. Such adventitious finds would be repeated as tea rooms tore away the Victorian-era renovations of eighteenth-century buildings, exposing rafters and finding fireplaces with their cranes and trammels still intact. Two sisters in Pennsylvania began a tea room in an old building that had never been remodeled. At first they felt ashamed that they lacked the funds to cover over the exposed ceiling beams, but they soon discovered that their guests were fascinated by them. Later they opened up a closed fireplace and found ancient andirons and an old crane and kettle warmer. So many guests asked them if they had any antiques to sell that they decided it was their "duty" to sell their own furnishings. When those were gone, they turned to neighbors for more. Quaint interiors supplied an excellent background for an antiques business, and many tea rooms made a practice of displaying antique furniture

LATHAM TEA ROOM LINCOLN ILL. 962
WHERE ABRAHAM LINCOLN WAS A FREQUENT GUEST

or tableware by letting patrons use these items. Visitors were sometimes surprised when other guests bought a hooked rug from the floor or carried off the table they had been sitting at.

Other Sorts of "Oldeness"

The absence of an available historic house or tavern did not mean a tea room proprietor had to forsake a claim to ye olden days. In the rapidly urbanizing and industrializing American society of the early twentieth century, barns and mills seemed ancient—even when they had operated rather recently in their original capacity. Old-time charm could also be squeezed out of other odd, sometimes unlikely, structures or imported into interiors of almost any building.

There developed a kind of loose "old English" style that was often found in city tea rooms. When in the form of dark paneling, hunting prints, and silver, it was presented as an upscale version of the Colonial style. At other times it was scarcely distinguishable from the standard Early American or Colonial types. In 1918 the staff of *Good Housekeeping* was especially fond of a "quaint" English tea room near Broadway in New York City that was also popular with artists, actors, and writers. It was decorated with chintz curtains, shelves with platters and teapots, and a fireplace hung with cooking implements. Greenwich Village's Pig 'n Whistle referred to its "Quaint Dickensonian Atmosphere," but the interior of its brownstone was as plain as a prison dining hall, perhaps representing another version of English quaintness.

Other sources of "oldeness" were there to be found if the tea room proprietor looked hard enough. Precedents for re-creating historic tableaus around eating went back to the 1860s. During the Civil War, Northern women had organized "sanitary fairs" to raise money for wounded soldiers. At these fairs they had presented historical teas and meals in decorated period rooms staffed by guides and waitresses costumed in Knickerbocker, Pennsylvania Dutch, or Old New England fashion. Old Dutch motifs reappeared in tea rooms, especially in the pre–World War I tea rooms of New York City. Later, in 1930, the Dutch Treat Tea Room on West Forty-ninth Street featured "real" Pennsylvania Dutch cooking. The Sunset Tea Room in Connecticut had a Dutch theme with waitresses dressed to match. Near Mount Holyoke College in South Hadley, Massachusetts, the Croysdale Inn contained several tea rooms and dining rooms, one with a Japanese theme, one with a Dutch theme, and one with an English theme. Japanese tea rooms were almost never (if ever) run by Asians. (Dutch and Japanese themes were ipso facto quaint, as no one could imagine these cultural iconographies as modern.) New

Tea Room

GEO. H. NEWTON
MANAGER

Prince George Hotel

5TH Avenue and 28TH Street
New York

THE TEA ROOM AT THE PRINCE GEORGE HOTEL WAS FURNISHED WITH WICKER CHAIRS AND LOUNGES GROUPED UNDER AN ARBOR OF TRELLISES AND VINES.

MANY OF THE HOSTESSES AT GREENWICH VILLAGE'S PEPPER POT WERE ART AND MUSIC STUDENTS AT NEW YORK UNIVERSITY. EACH WEARS THE VIRTUAL VILLAGE UNIFORM OF THE 1920S, THE ARTIST'S SMOCK.

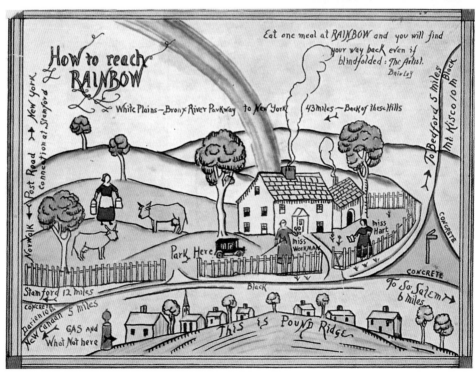

RIGHT: TEA ROOMS WERE POPULAR
DESTINATIONS FOR WEEKEND TOURING PARTIES,
AS DEPICTED IN THIS 1927 KELLY-SPRINGFIELD
TIRE ADVERTISEMENT.
(GOODYEAR TIRE & RUBBER COMPANY)

BELOW: THE RAINBOW TEA HOUSE IN POUND
RIDGE, NEW YORK, CLEARLY EXPECTED GUESTS
TO ARRIVE BY CAR FROM CITIES FAR AND NEAR.

TOP: THE PROPRIETORS POSE IN FRONT OF THEIR PRIM-LOOKING LIGHT HOUSE SERVICE STATION AND TEA ROOM IN HENRYVILLE, PENNSYLVANIA.

LEFT: ALTHOUGH THE WHISTLING OYSTER TEA ROOM WAS CLOSED ON SUNDAY, THIS WAS A PRIME BUSINESS DAY FOR MOST ROADSIDE TEA ROOMS.

RIGHT: IN ITS EARLY DAYS THE ROSLYN MILL TEA HOUSE ON LONG ISLAND, LOCATED IN A HISTORIC GRISTMILL, WAS OPERATED BY ALICE TITUS.

BELOW LEFT: A CAREFULLY COMPOSED MEDITERRANEAN SALAD OF GRAPEFRUIT AND ORANGE SECTIONS, GARNISHED WITH MAYONNAISE.

BELOW RIGHT: THE TOMATO SURPRISE, USUALLY FILLED WITH CHICKEN SALAD, WAS ONE OF THE MOST POPULAR TEA ROOM DISHES. THE SALAD IS SHOWN HERE ON A TYPICAL TEA ROOM GREEN-GLASS PLATE.

Tea at the Old Mill Roslyn

Mediterranean Salad

Tomato Surprise (page 14)

PURITAN   MADELON

LEFT: A COUPLE OF THE FOURTEEN COLORFUL WAITRESS UNIFORMS SUITABLE FOR TEA ROOMS FEATURED IN A 1929 CATALOG. THE ORCHID APRONETTE SHOWN WITH THE MADELON "STRIKES A CHARMING NOTE OF COLOR," ACCORDING TO THE CATALOG COPY.

BELOW: STYLISHLY MODERNE MATCHCOVER FOR THE RISMONT TEA ROOM CHAIN IN NEW YORK CITY.

THE ORANGE-AND-BLACK INTERIOR OF THE PHEASANT COFFEE SHOPPE IN PROVIDENCE, RHODE ISLAND. ALTHOUGH CALLED A COFFEE SHOP, THE PHEASANT HAD A STEREOTYPICAL TEA ROOM LOOK, SERVED AFTERNOON TEA, AND CATERED TO BRIDGE PARTIES.

THE BLUE PARROT TEA ROOM IN GETTYSBURG, PENNSYLVANIA, DISPLAYED THE MULTICOLORED LOOK BRILLIANTLY. A PARROT MOTIF ADORNS A LAMPSHADE AND A BLACK PILLOW.

THE ITALIAN TEA GARDEN AT THE MARY LOUISE IN LOS ANGELES, WHERE A FESTIVE ATMOSPHERE WAS CREATED WITH STRIPED TENTING, CHAIRS OF MANY COLORS, AND JAPANESE LANTERNS.

TOP: THE OWNERS OF THE GYPSY
INN IN ST. PETERSBURG, FLORIDA,
DESCRIBED IT AS "A VERITABLE
BOHEMIA IN ALL THAT WORD
IMPLIES." THE CLASSIC 1920S TEA
ROOM INTERIOR DISPLAYS A
DRAPED SHAWL, CANDLES,
GRILLWORK, GYPSY COSTUMES,
WATER JUGS AND LANTERNS, AS
WELL AS APPLE-GREEN SHELVES,
WINDSOR CHAIRS, AND SETTLES. ALL
THAT IS MISSING IS A PARROT.

LEFT: A SOPHISTICATED POSTCARD
ADVERTISING THE HOCHSCHILD,
KOHN AND COMPANY DEPARTMENT
STORE TEA ROOM IN BALTIMORE.

"WHERE GOOD DIGESTION WAITS ON APPETITE"

The TEA ROOM
AT HOCHSCHILD, KOHN & CO'S.

RIGHT: CHILDREN'S MENU FROM THE TEA ROOM AT O'NEIL'S DEPARTMENT STORE, AKRON, OHIO.

BOTTOM LEFT: POSTER STAMP PUBLICIZING THE TEA ROOMS IN THE GLASS BLOCK DEPARTMENT STORE, DULUTH, MINNESOTA, CIRCA 1914.

BOTTOM RIGHT: 1920S MENU COVER FROM THE LASALLE AND KOCH TEA ROOMS IN TOLEDO, OHIO. MANAGED BY MABEL LITTLE, THE DEPARTMENT-STORE TEA ROOMS WERE KNOWN FOR THEIR MODISH MODERN DECOR.

York City's Rooftree Inn on West Twenty-eighth Street advertised in 1927 that it featured "the charm of the New York of yesteryear and the delights of the old time home kitchen," indicating that a city's history could also furnish a link to a golden past. The Old Kaufmann House in "Historic Nauvoo, Illinois" was home to the Dutch Oven Tea Room, a name found also in Greenwich Village and Northampton, Massachusetts.

Mills and barns were perennially popular sites for tea rooms. "Do You Own a Barn, an Old Mill or a Tumble-Down House?" asked the title of a *Woman's Home Companion* tea room story in May 1922. "Cash Value Found in Old-Time Settings" an article in *Tea Room and Gift Shop* informed its subscribers the following year. Helen M. Woods, entrepreneur of the Tea Room Training Organization, advised in her promotional brochure that prospective tea room owners use what they had, whether it be a porch, basement, or front garden, adding, "I almost forgot to mention the wonderful possibilities of an old mill."

Mills often made up for their rather nondescript interiors by their links to a bygone energy source and their picturesque location on a river

INTERIOR OF THE TEA
BARN AROUND 1925,
ON WEST MAIN STREET
IN HYANNIS,
MASSACHUSETTS.

or stream. On Martha's Vineyard, the Old Mill in West Tisbury served a number of purposes in its retirement, including a tea room, sandwich shop, art gallery, and auction house. Ye Olde Mill Tea House, built in 1724 near Hatboro, Pennsylvania, was rescued from a machine shop and restored by an architect. When its floor was replaced with broad pine boards, they were aged with rubbed-in dirt, showing how oldness sometimes had to be coaxed. On Long Island, the long-lived Roslyn Tea Room was located in a gristmill built in 1701. Under the huge rough-hewn ceiling beams, guests, including many from the theatrical world, ate at candlelit tables that ranged from dainty gateleg to long, rustic trestle styles.

Windmills went other mills one better in quaintness and were sought-after locations for tea rooms and roadside gift shops. In July 1926 a woman named Margaret drove to Cape Cod with six friends to eat lunch at the House of the Wind Mill Tea Room in Cataumet. Sitting on a glassed-in porch at the back of the windmill, overlooking a pond, she wrote to a friend in Paris, asking if she too was seeing "picturesque things." The House of the Wind Mill was run by a graduate of the Washington, D.C.–based Lewis Tea Room Training Course and was pictured in a 1923 promotional brochure as a "quaint 'down east' tea room." The windmill of the Old Dutch Tea Room beckoned to motorists driving on the Schaghticoke Trail along the Housatonic River in Connecticut. In Southampton, Long Island, the Old Hayground Windmill, built in 1801, was alternately used as a tea room and an artist's studio after it ceased operation as a gristmill in 1919.

Barns closely rivaled mills as picturesque locations for tea rooms and were often decorated with hay and pitchforks. One of the best known was the Whipple Tea Barn in North Pownal, Vermont. The 150-year-old barn was operated in the 1920s by a member of the fifth generation of Whipples, descendants of a Revolutionary War soldier who once operated a

YE NAMES

Ye Mayflower Tea Room,
San Francisco

Ye Kyng's Towne Sweetes,
Kingston, Massachusetts

Ye Olde Fashioned Tea Shoppe,
Madison, Wisconsin

Ye Olde Tea House,
Stone Harbor, New Jersey

Ye Rose Tree Inn,
Northampton, Massachusetts

Ye Pollywogge, Greenwich Village

Ye Olde Spinning Wheele,
Tavares, Florida

Ye Township Tea Room,
Washington, D.C.

Ye Candle Glow, Norwich, Vermont

Ye Olde Mill Tea House,
Hatboro, Pennsylvania

Ye Little Hatchet Tavern,
Mount Vernon, Virginia

Ye Green Lantern Inn,
Hanover, New Hampshire

Ye Olde Brick Shoppe, Lyndon,
Vermont

Ye Stockade Tea Room,
Deerfield, Massachusetts

Ye Olde Virginnie, McKenney, Virginia

Ye Old Harmony Tavern,
New York City

Ye Olde Village Inn,
South Orange, New Jersey

Ye Pig 'n Whistle Inn, Greenwich Village

Ye Olde Wayside Inne,
Scarsdale, New York

Ye Olde McCormick Tea House,
Baltimore, Maryland

Ye Olde Colonial T-House,
Ridgefield, Connecticut

Ye Olde English Tea Rooms,
South Hadley, Massachusetts

Ye Set-A-Spell Tea House,
location unknown

Ye Peggy Stewart Tea Room, Baltimore

stagecoach inn on the property. Next to the barn, tables were arranged under a pergola with an unusual top fashioned from hay. The tea room was on the "Ideal Automobile Tour" between Troy, New York, and North Adams, Massachusetts, and drew motorists from afar as well as townspeople from nearby Bennington. The Yellow Hen, in Plainfield, New Jersey, was in an old chicken barn, expensively remodeled in 1921 with hardwood floors and drop lighting over each table. In Aiken, South Carolina, the Barn Tea Room offered cozy seating inside a well-furnished living room with a view of a civilized-looking pond bordered by flowers and visited by flamingos.

No old building was too odd to house a tea room. The decline in horse-drawn transportation freed up stables and harness shops that were snapped up for tea rooms. The Wenham Village Improvement Society in Massachusetts rented an old harness shop for its tea room in 1912, paying $5 a month in rent. Numerous city tea rooms were located in former stables, the most famed being the Tally-Ho in New York City, where dining in a horse stall proved to be something to write home about. Stables proved so popular that, by 1928, they were no longer cheap to rent in some locations. In Greenwich Village an abandoned stable was said to be "worth the weight of its wide gates in pure gold" by 1928. Tea rooms were also established in other unusual locations such as a tollhouse (Betty Benz, Nantucket), a shipyard (Sandpiper Inn and Tea Room, Madison, Connecticut), a church (Chapel Inn, Duarte, California), and a bowling alley (Old Bowling Alley Tea House, Princeton, Massachusetts).

The Skipper Tea House, opened on Nantucket in 1920, was housed partially on an old coal boat and partially in an old laundry building at which the boat was docked. Prior to operating as a laundry the building had had a diverse life as a Quaker meetinghouse and as a merry-go-round shelter. In another sign of recycling, the proprietors (a Smith College

THE OLD HORSE STALLS
AT THE IRON GATE
INN, IN WASHINGTON,
D.C., STILL BORE THE
NAMES OF GOLDEN
PEBBLES AND OLD EBB,
TWO FORMER EQUINE
RESIDENTS.

graduate and her California friend) used the boat's engine to cool their ice cream freezer. The Skipper's patrons included old sea captains, Main Street ladies, celebrities from the village of Sconset, and flappers and athletes from the yacht club. At 3 P.M. story hour began, and patrons could sign up for a series of ten story hours, with refreshments, for $10.

Not "Olde," Just Quaint

New buildings often borrowed from past styles, and tea rooms were frequently located in new structures inspired by the Colonial Revival, the

Mission Revival, and other styles influenced by the Arts & Crafts movement. In Michigan, near Detroit, a mother-and-daughter team ran the MacDiarmid Homestead and Colonial Tea Room in 1914 in a newly built Colonial Revival building modeled on the Craigie House near Cambridge, Massachusetts. A replica of the Abraham Lincoln home in Springfield, Illinois, that was built for the 1905 Lewis and Clark Centennial Exposition in Portland, Oregon, had an interesting career after the fair ended. The house was rented out and deteriorated, then was bought by a developer, who cut it in half and moved it, whereupon the half moved to Twentieth Street became a tea room for a time. New York City's Ye Peg Woffington Coffee House (one of the many tea rooms called a coffeehouse), caught the attention of architects when it was depicted in leading trade magazines in 1924. Designed by Richard Haviland Smythe, the Tudor-style interior featured rough plaster and exposed brick walls, half-timbering and exposed roof trusses, and leaded-glass casement windows. The built-in wooden booths "carry out the suggestion of informality and comfort to perfection," said an architectural journal, especially since the design allowed for so many corner seats (which, the architect said, made customers feel secure).

Romantic retro styles in California took other directions. In Carmel-by-the-Sea, one of the many buildings designed in the 1920s by local architect Hugh Comstock was destined to achieve iconic status as the Tuck Box Tea Room, established in the early 1940s and living on into the twenty-first century. Comstock designed his first building, his own home, in the 1920s. Its cottagey charms were so strong that others in Carmel begged him to build one for them. He designed the wobbly-looking half-timbered cottage that became the

Quaint Tea Room

Accommodations for Tourists

Mrs. Harris J. Myers
West Winfield, N. Y.

PHONE 92-F-2.

Jane's Cake Shop and English Tea Room
Carmel by the Sea, Calif.

zf 355

Tuck Box in 1927, either as his office or as a shop where his wife, May-otta, could sell the "Otsy-Totsy" dolls she made. In the early 1930s the building was used as Sally's Restaurant, and in the late 1930s, Pearl Ridg-ley and Mae Crawford used it as the Blue Bird Tea Room.

Lilian Rice, one of the first three women to receive a degree in archi-tecture at the University of California, Berkeley, in 1927 designed the Stu-dio Shop and Tea Room, part of the Rancho Santa Fe planned community in San Diego, for which she was supervisory architect. Rice had briefly been a draftswoman for architect Hazel Waterman, who in 1910 super-vised restoration of the Casa de Estudillo, known popularly as "Ramona's marriage place," after the 1884 novel *Ramona*. Rice would draw on this work when she designed La Amapola (The Poppy), as the Studio Tea Room was known. Situated in an inner courtyard, with a tiled patio in front, it occupied a large room with a fireplace, which was an exact replica of the one at Ramona's marriage place. The tea room was run by Marie Ketchum, the wife of Rancho Santa Fe's building contractor. At its grand opening in June of 1928, its stucco Mission-style interior niches were filled with poppies and other flowers in an orange, blue, and yellow color scheme. One hundred and fifty guests were serenaded by a woman singing and playing Spanish songs on a guitar. La Amapola catered bridge parties and sold handmade peasant crafts such as Mexican glassware, wrought-iron items, and Native American pottery.

❖ ❖ ❖

Colonial themes were popular in big-city tea rooms all over the country, especially in the 1930s Depression when this style promised security and comfort. Soon this decor would spread beyond tea rooms to all types of eating—*and drinking*—places. After Prohibition ended in 1933, Colonial decor made the full circle from eighteenth-century tavern to twentieth-century tavern as bar owners discovered that women much preferred to drink cocktails in Early American barrooms rather than in those with streamlined moderne styling that architects and interior designers advocated.

Even as the Colonial style spread, its meaning gradually drained away. The reverence that early tea room owners had for the Colonial past, with all it represented to them, made many turn against this style when it became too widespread. As early as 1928 criticism was leveled against old-fashioned-looking tea rooms that were decorated to the hilt, but invested little in their cuisine. "The lady in a southwestern city, who stuck a spinning wheel in her tea room window, and bought the pies and cakes at a bakery may wonder why she failed. I don't," declared Cecil Reams frankly. Frances Hunt, another critic, said that those who stopped at "The Blue China Teapot, The Cheering Cup, and the Sign of the Steaming Samovar" often left feeling "the gift shop is the real point of the whole operation." The word *Colonial*, said one tea room correspondence course in 1932, had been used so often and so inappropriately, it no longer had real meaning. Indeed, in 1936 the Colonial Tea Room in Niagara Falls sported a vaguely art deco interior and had a cocktail lounge.

The tea room, whose women proprietors had so often disavowed a merely mercenary motive, was becoming commercial. The urban tea room would develop its potential as a moneymaker as chains evolved in the late 1920s and the 1930s, many neither owned nor managed by women.

CHAPTER FIVE

Metropolitan Meals

Who ever sees a stenographer carrying her lunch nowadays?
She gets her food in the Tea Room now.

—TEA ROOM AND GIFT SHOP, JANUARY 1923

By the 1920s the tea room was a recognized national insti-tution, with its stronghold on the main streets of cities, towns, and suburbs. It was a popular rendezvous for work-ing women, shoppers, and businessmen, as well as whole families eating their evening meal. The eating-out public was growing rapidly in the post–World War I period, as women joined the workforce, urban populations grew, and increasing numbers of people spent all day away from home.

The male-dominated restaurant industry, which had formed only recently, grudgingly acknowledged that tea rooms and women diners were something to reckon with. Women formed an estimated 60 percent of restaurant patrons by the mid-1920s, up from about 20 percent in 1917. And the tea room, however small potatoes it was in its ability to purchase expensive restaurant equipment, was clearly the type of restaurant women preferred. Restaurant industry consultant Joseph Dahl admitted in 1927 that the average restaurant operator lacked the motivation to please female patrons "until thoughtful women started to compete for this business and take it from him."

A tea room industry began to emerge, with companies providing tailored products and services. High school, college, and correspondence courses abounded, training women on topics such as quantity food buying and preparation, advertising, and personnel management. Correspondence courses were offered by the Lewis Tea Room Institute, Helen Woods, and the Women's Institute of Scranton, Pennsylvania. Alice Bradley, cooking editor of *Woman's Home Companion* and director of Miss [Fanny] Farmer's School of Cookery in Boston, wrote a correspondence course book titled *Cooking for Profit*. "A common method of determining the selling price of cooked food is to double the cost of the raw material. Can you get this price?" she asked her readers. Students at Miss Farmer's could study tea room management as part of a one-year course or learn tea room cookery. Sisters Josephine and Jeannette Ware, successful proprietors of the tea-

ADVERTISEMENT FOR A ST. LOUIS TEA SHOP THAT APPEARED IN A 1930 MUNICIPAL OPERA PROGRAM.

CAMILLE TEA SHOPPE
6163-65 Delmar

Bridge Parties
Luncheons
''Dinners''
CAMILLE E. PREISS
Cabany 6147

TEA AT THE BLUE LANTERN INN

New Poise and Charm for You

Not the least fascinating of the many delightful features of this wonderful industry is the manner in which it helps you to acquire personal poise and charm—that subtle something called "personality." You will soon find yourself meeting strangers with perfect ease, displaying a grace in deportment and conversation which will astonish you. Miss Gertrude Farrell, who conducts the Harvard Tea Room in a rustic Massachusetts village, comments on this point: "We meet splendid people," she says. "Often we entertain a celebrity of the stage or screen or someone else of public interest. Our guests take almost a personal interest in our attractive little place." A certain delightful poise and charm seem to characterize the tea room hostess, regardless of age.

room-by-another-name, the Ware Coffee House on Beekman Street in New York City, ran the Ware School of Tea Room Management in 1924. While teaching students about the intricacies of bookkeeping, they undoubtedly implanted their credo: "That woman's place is in the tea-room has been accepted as an inevitable corollary of 'woman's place is in the home.'"

Books, journals, and employment agencies began to appear. Foremost among cookbooks was *Tea-Room Recipes* by Lenore Richards and Nola Treat, published in 1925. The authors, who ran the genteel, tea-room-like Richards-Treat Cafeteria in Minneapolis, provided quantity recipes for dishes like cold chicken mousse with asparagus and creamed mushrooms on toast. A restaurant trade magazine devoted to tea rooms was started. *Tea-Room Management* (later changing its name to *Tea Room and Gift Shop*, then to *Restaurant and Tea Room Journal*) commenced in August of 1922, suddenly

LEFT: FROM "POURING TEA FOR PROFIT," A LEWIS TEA ROOM INSTITUTE PROMOTIONAL BROCHURE, CIRCA 1923.

RIGHT: ADVERTISEMENT APPEARING IN *HOUSE BEAUTIFUL*, MARCH 1926.

and inexplicably folding in July of 1925. It featured few recipes, focusing mainly on success stories, not all of them completely convincing. Nevertheless, its departure at a time when the number of tea rooms was expanding left a hole that was filled by tea room articles in mainstream journals such as *Restaurant Management* and *The American Restaurant*. Other services to tea rooms included employment agencies that specialized in providing trained workers, among them the McDermott Hotel, Tea Room and Restaurant Employment Agency, and the Elizabeth Arnold Employment Service in Cleveland, Ohio. Along with tea room managers, the Arnold agency also placed club executives, dietitians, cafeteria managers, hostesses, home economics teachers, and school-lunch managers—other burgeoning food-related careers that attracted women in the 1920s.

Tea rooms were buyers of imported goods as varied as Asian lanterns and Italian pottery, but they also bought American-made tablewares for use. Especially popular were sets of glass dishes in green, pink, amber, and clear produced for tea rooms by the Indiana Glass Company from 1926 to 1931. In a tiered art deco pattern called Tea Room, the line included a great variety of pieces, such as plates and cups, pickle dishes, platters, glasses, sugars and creamers, candlesticks, vases, lamp bases, and a range of ice cream service dishes.

Twentieth-Century Boom

The oldest urban tea rooms dated back to the 1890s, but were few in number. In Boston and other cities, women's exchanges served afternoon tea, along with lunch and dinner. But no more than a handful of tea rooms were known in New York City or Boston in the 1890s, even by contemporaries like temperance advocate Frances Willard, who was always on the lookout for alcohol-free zones for gentlewomen.

The twentieth century saw major growth, though occurring slowly at first. In Boston, before 1910, tea drinkers could go to the Art Lunch or to Miss Preble's. A visitor to Miss Preble's Lunch and Tea Rooms on Boylston Street in 1907 reported that she stopped there to celebrate after a concert at the nearby Christian Science Church. The Art Lunch and Tea Room was started next to the public library in Copley Square in 1905 by a Miss Pinkham. Patrons dining in the comfortable-looking rooms at the Blagden Street brownstone could enjoy "home-cooked" chicken, steak, or chops from mid-September to June. In 1905 at DeKlyn's, on Euclid Avenue in Cleveland, downtown shoppers whiled away "those dull afternoons" as they listened to music and consumed "her majesty's tea with English crumpets, tea cake, crisp toast, Scotch scones, German coffee cake," among other international delicacies. The Chesterfield Tea Room was established in 1903 in Richmond, Virginia. Like another early Southern tea room, the Satsuma in Nashville, Tennessee, it would become a local institution.

In other cities, early tea rooms included the prewar Egyptian Tea Room on Morrison Street in Portland, Oregon, located at the back of the Royal Bakery and Confectionery. In Pasadena, an English tea house called the Hob and Toasting Fork was in business in 1910. In Hartford, Connecticut, the Colonial Tea Shop was in operation on Pratt Street in 1915. In Greeneville, Tennessee, a rest room for women visiting the town was created in 1910 out of an

AROUND 1910 THE GREEN DRAGON MOVED FROM TWENTY-SECOND STREET TO THIS NEW ADDRESS.

SIGN OF THE GREEN DRAGON
LUNCHEON AND TEA ROOM

5 East 36th Street, New York
TELEPHONE 2887 MAD. SQ.

eight-room house, with one room reserved for a tea room and another for a reading room. Women in Springfield, Massachusetts, in 1914 could have tea or lunch in the tea room that was part of the Washington Lunch. In La Jolla, California, diners could in 1918 enjoy the unusual experience of eating in the Dining Car Tea Shop, fashioned from an old streetcar. In New Orleans, Kolb's German restaurant devoted its second floor to a tea room as early as 1914. The Copper Kettle, at 233 Mercantile Place, claimed to be Los Angeles' first tea room, begun sometime before the First World War.

The war brought more people to cities and greatly increased the number of eating places of all kinds, including tea rooms. Boston, which by 1918 had 510 eating places, was said to be "well supplied" with tea rooms then. During the war, when women came to the city for government jobs, Washington, D.C., experienced a surge of "artistically furnished" tea rooms, mostly in the Lafayette Square area. The city's first tea room was the Asian-styled Lotos Lantern, established in 1914 by two sisters from Virginia. Nashville's Satsuma was started by two domestic-

"THE INTERIOR IS FASCINATING," WROTE KATE TO A FRIEND IN MASSACHUSETTS ON THIS POSTCARD AFTER VISITING THE ROSE TREE TEA HOUSE IN PASADENA IN 1914. "THEY HAVE A FEW ITALIAN THINGS FOR SALE, BESIDE MARMALADE AND JELLY. FOOD DELICIOUS."

A QUIET CORNER OF THE LOTOS LANTERN TEA ROOM, 733 SEVENTEENTH STREET, WASHINGTON, D. C.

science teachers in 1918. In Chicago's Loop there were numerous tea rooms on and around Michigan Avenue by 1920, many on upper floors of office buildings. Tea rooms in Chicago were also plentiful in residential neighborhoods, often in houses or the basements of apartment buildings. In 1925, over eighty places with *tea* in their name were listed in the Chicago telephone directory. Philadelphia listed about thirty in 1925. San Francisco evidently had few early tea rooms. A 1929 survey of over eleven hundred eating places in San Francisco found only twenty tea rooms, fewer than in a single city block in New York's "roaring forties" then. Twenty-nine tea rooms lined West Forty-ninth Street between Fifth and Sixth Avenues circa 1928, constituting but a small fraction of the hundreds that existed in the city.

Tea rooms tended to develop loyal patrons, and many became institutions in their town or city. Prominent among these was the Maramor in Columbus, Ohio, established in the early 1920s by Mary Love McGuckin. Regarded as one of the best restaurants in the country in the 1940s, a guest reported to *Gourmet's Guide*, "You will get so many letters about this

place that no comment from me will be needed." Among its other fans
were Eddie Cantor (who sent a telegram that said, "My body is in
Rochester, but my appetite is at the Maramor"), and Alfred Lunt and Lynn
Fontanne, who had a dish named for them (Lamb Luntanne). The
Maramor is almost certainly the restaurant that Gertrude Stein and Alice B.
Toklas visited in 1934, and that Alice remembered fondly in her 1954
cookbook. It "served meals that would have been my pride if they had
come to our table from our kitchen," she said. The Tick Tock Tea Room,
established in Hollywood, California in 1931, played a similar role for its
patrons, as did the Frances Virginia on Peachtree Street in Atlanta, the
Kirby Allen and Mary Elizabeth's in New York City, the Parkway in
Chicago, and Damon's in Cleveland Heights.

Location, Location, Location

Since an urban tea room drew most of its customers from lunch crowds, its location was of critical importance. Desirable locations included near a large hotel, railroad station, place of amusement, or school, or inside an office building. Many were situated in the heart of a city's shopping district. The Ardzli Tea Room on Sixth Street in Portsmouth, Ohio, was near a courthouse, post office, banks, and bus and streetcar lines. Alice Foote MacDougall's Cortile, inside an office building on West Forty-third Street in New York City, was near Stern Brothers department store, the Aeolian

THE NAME OF THE ARDZLI TEA ROOM IN PORTSMOUTH, OHIO, WAS MADE BY COMBINING THE SECOND SYLLABLES OF THE LAST NAMES OF THE TWO OWNERS, WILLARD AND KUENZLI.

Hall, and the Hippodrome, as well as theaters on Fifth Avenue. In Chicago, the Picadilly Tea Room was located on the fourth floor of the Fine Arts Building on Michigan Boulevard. It used the roof of the neighboring Studebaker Theatre as the floor of its courtyard, where a fountain was surrounded by tea tables with striped umbrellas. The Atlantic Theatre and Tea Room were run in conjunction in Spring Lake, New Jersey, in the 1920s, while the Highgate Hall Tea Room operated in the Bellevue Theater Building in Upper Montclair. In 1925 the Wisteria Tea Garden was located on East State Street in Ithaca, New York, opposite the Strand Theatre, and offered "dainty food served in a fastidious manner." Ann Heyneman's Tea Room, at 449 Mason Street in San Francisco, was close to shopping and theaters in the mid-1930s.

In New York City, locations in the Thirty-third Street shopping district proved popular for tea rooms such as the Cosy, the Chimney Corner, the Fernery, and the Colonia in the midteens. The Women's Suffrage party headquarters and tea shop chose a location at 38 East Thirty-fourth Street in 1913, while At the Sign of the Green Parrot was located opposite Altman's on Thirty-fifth Street in 1916. Mary Elizabeth's Tea Room and Restaurant, on the corner of Fifth Avenue and Thirty-sixth Street, was situated in a fashionable shopping area with Altman's, Best & Co., Lord & Taylor, and Franklin-Simon's.

An address in an affluent suburb also worked well for tea rooms. Women, it was said, "abandoned cooking" in the 1920s, a fact often cited as a reason for increased dining out by women, married couples, and families. One forlorn man was overheard complaining to another in 1922 that his wife went to bridge parties every afternoon and would not cook. "She just runs around to the delicatessen shop half an hour before I get home. If ever I complain of growing tired of such grub, she says something about not marrying me to be a cook, or that she needs social life as much as I need food." *Tea Room and Gift Shop* noted in 1923 that eating out as well as giving parties in hotels and tea rooms was a sign that the modern woman was achieving freedom from "the rigid bondage that once held her in complete subjection." A women's manifesto published in *Woman's Home Companion* in 1923 presented a resolution: "That it is the duty of the women of this country to free themselves from irrational drudgery for the sake of their higher duties as wives, mothers, and as individuals."

Aware of their mission to replace the home dining room, suburban tea rooms strove to be as "tastefully" decorated as an upper-middle-class home. By the mid-1920s a residential tea room displaying good taste would have small rooms with buff-colored stucco walls connected by gracefully arched doorways. Large windows would be covered with sheer draperies, and soft, indirect lighting would be supplied by wall sconces. Furniture might be the ever-popular Windsor chairs and gateleg tables or of the newly popular Mediterranean style. Such interiors could be found at Polly's Patio Tea Shop in the 1920s. Polly's, at West Seventh and Shatto Place, advertised that it was located "in the heart of Los Angeles' finest residential section." The description might have applied as well to Grace Smith's Ottawa Hills Tea House, which was located at the intersection of five paved roads, in "the heart of the most exclusive suburban residence section." Ten minutes outside Toledo, Ohio, Ottawa Hills was a parklike residential development of the midteens, with a lake, boathouse, tennis courts, winding roads, and "sylvan paths." Grace Smith said that she tried to make her tea house as homelike as possible. "We use luncheon cloths and doilies in blue cross-stitch at noon and the formal linen cloths and napkins at night and, in short, try to do everything as one would like it in her own home," she explained in 1922.

Homelike tea rooms in suburban settings, sometimes in the proprietor's own home, were found throughout the country in the 1920s and

1930s. The Betty Bolton, in Hollywood, California, was operated in 1922 by the son and daughter-in-law of songwriter Carrie Jacobs Bond, renowned for the hit "I Love You Truly." The Original Brooke Tea House in Takoma Park, Maryland, was said to be the first suburban tea house outside Washington, D.C. In Glendale, California, patrons in the 1920s could choose among the Forget-Me-Not on South Central, the Ideal Tea Room and the Harvard Tea Room on Central, or the Glendale Garden on North Glendale. The Forget-Me-Not stayed open on Christmas Day in 1928 and served a complete dinner with Waldorf salad, turkey, squash, and fruitcake, all for $1.25.

Women in Chicago's suburbs must have vacated their kitchens en masse because these towns seemed to have had a special abundance of tea rooms. The Green Tea Pot, begun in 1922 by Carrie M. Green, had three locations: one in Highland Park, one in Lake Forest, and the third in Waukegan. Other Chicago suburban tea rooms, in 1931, included three Evanston locations of Cooley's Cupboards, the Homestead and Madeline Mehlig's Tea Shop in Evanston, and the Hearthstone on Linden Avenue in Hubbard Woods. Oak Park had both the Windsor Tea Room and Mrs. Maynard's Community Kitchen, the latter one of three tea rooms operated by Mrs. Maynard. Oak Park was also the location of the Three Sisters Tea Room, which was indeed operated by three sisters, old hands from Chicago restaurant days before the war. Wilhemina Howland rented a

Frank Lloyd Wright house on the north side of Chicago, at 7631 Sheridan Road, for her Black Oak Tea Room. Seeking a clientele who loved "good food and cultured atmosphere," she specialized in mushrooms under glass and chicken. In 1931, lunch there cost $1.50 and up and dinner was a pricey $1.50 to $2.50.

Women, Children, and Men

Catering to whole families meant making children comfortable and reining in their energy for a hour or so, something most restaurants didn't want to deal with. Atlanta's Frances Virginia Tea Room, like many others, designed a special children's menu that could be worn as a mask. After the children finished their meal, the Frances Virginia presented them with a box of animal crackers. Other tea rooms had menus with puzzles and games to help children endure the long session at the table. Paying attention to children's needs, insisted one tea room proprietor, meant that the children would suggest going back to the tea room next time.

Of course, in urban tea rooms as elsewhere, women were the basic clientele. While they catered to women of leisure, who often spent afternoons playing bridge or mah-jongg at tea rooms, they also had many workingwomen patrons. Just like workingmen, these patrons had to watch the clock and return to their desks promptly. Mary Elizabeth's in New York City decided to concentrate on salads, croquettes, and other dishes that could be served quickly rather than competing with slow-service hotels on things like lobster, roasts, or steaks. Gertrude Hastings saw to it that her tea room on the ground floor of Chicago's Insurance Ex-

change Building met the needs of working girls. She had previously been a bookkeeper at an insurance company in a neighborhood where there were no good places for office women to eat. She advertised her tea room by distributing thousands of cards to girls working in nearby offices and, in 1920, served about fourteen hundred meals a day. In Seattle in 1923 a tea room for working-women was located in the Metropolitan Building and specialized in ready dishes such as creamed tuna, creamed chicken, and olive and mayonnaise sandwiches.

Workingwomen's ability to afford tea room prices owed everything to a rising standard of living in the postwar 1920s. Still, it was a stretch for some women. Sociologist Frances Donovan took a job in a New York department store to gather material for her analysis of workingwomen. She made a friend at the store, Edith, and they often went out to lunch together. At a tea room on Forty-seventh Street, they had a table d'hôte lunch of soup, meat, potatoes, and vegetables for 50¢. If they ate at a lunch counter, by contrast, they could get a sandwich and cup of tea for only 20¢. While the tea room furnished a full meal, it cost more than twice as much as the average quick lunch, but it appealed to Edith because it offered more of a respite from workday pressures. Frances was a bit shocked when her friend told her she had to choose between buying clothes or paying the rent, and even more so when Frances went to Edith's apartment and discovered that it was in a tenement, with a metal washtub in the kitchen serving for a bathtub.

During the early 1930s, tea rooms were forced to reduce prices to stay in business. This was a boon for those workingwomen who still held jobs. In Allentown, Pennsylvania, the Colonial Luncheonette and Tea Room advertised that it was "at war with Mr. Business D. Pression" and offered 25¢ luncheons and free delivery to offices.

The Depression stimulated some tea rooms to turn away from quaintness (even as others clung to it). New York's Rismont Tea Room at Broadway near Fiftieth, designed by John Vassos circa 1931, was a large, streamlined eatery designed to feed office workers quickly and send them on their way. Its moderne black facade and red neon sign signaled a Depression-defying optimism and rejection of sentimental styles from the past. Larger size plus quicker turnover of customers in places like the Rismont, and in other tea room chains (there were three Rismonts), was a way to lower prices.

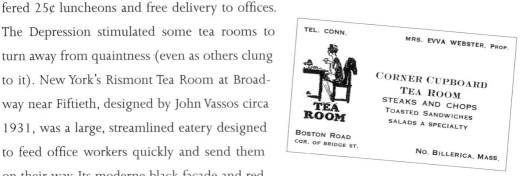

Candy, Soda Fountains, and Chains

Many city tea rooms were part of chains, a development that tended to leave women proprietors behind. There were a few exceptions among the female ranks, however. Alice Foote MacDougall flourished with six tea room/coffee shops in the 1920s, creating quite a stir in the business world when she signed a million-dollar lease for her Piazzetta on West Forty-seventh Street. Mary Elizabeth's, begun in 1908 as a self-service candy shop in Syracuse by Mary Elizabeth Evans, also signed a million-dollar lease for its Fifth Avenue and Thirty-sixth Street location, in the early 1920s. The amount "staggered everybody who knew us," admitted manager Fanny R. Evans in 1923. Mary Elizabeth's also had other locations, including a Tea House and Italian Garden at Greenacres at the Scarsdale Estates in Hartsdale, New York, in the teens, and a candy shop and tea room on Temple Place in Boston. In Chicago, Miss Ellis, a former steel company accountant, started her first tea room in 1910 and by 1929 had built a small chain, with her eighty-four-year-old mother serving as vice president. Her East Madison Street location was popular with commercial illustrators, such as Buster Brown creator R.F. Outcault, who decorated her walls with their original drawings. An energetic Grace Pebbles, evidently an early jet-setter, owned and managed tea rooms in 1941 in Chicago (Le Petit Gourmet), Evanston (Blue Parrot Patio), Hollywood (Gourmet Hollywood), Denver (Blue Parrot Inn), and Miami (Wishing Well). Numbers of other women tea room operators ran two or three places, but few exceeded this number.

Larger chains, like Boston's English Tea Rooms, were typically owned and managed by men. Manhattan-based Schrafft's, with forty-four outlets in the East by the mid-1940s, although started by Frank Shattuck, was heavily influenced in its development by his sister Jane. She served sandwiches and cakes that she made in Schrafft's second location at 54 West Twenty-third Street. By 1925 there were twenty-one locations in New York City, the chain's growth "largely due to Miss Shattuck's thorough understanding of the value of absolute cleanliness, daintiness, supreme food and cooking," according to the trade magazine *The Restaurateur*. The restaurants were originally exclusively for women, later expanding to male patronage. They remained a favorite with women, however. "Ask any woman...where she is going to lunch and the nearest Schrafft's is an odds-on favorite," reported a restaurant reviewer in 1925. In that year the restaurants were still conducted entirely by women, many of them college students in domestic science, working under Jane's supervision.

CATERING TO THE COLLEGE CROWD

College students were big tea room customers. Before pizza parlors, some tea rooms, such as the Walnut Street Tea Room in West Chester, Pennsylvania, delivered snacks to students at night. Others supplied breakfast to students who overslept their dormitory's mealtime. The Gingham Shop was three blocks from a state university with eight thousand students and found in the 1920s it had a ready supply of young people looking for waffles and toasted English muffins on Saturday and Sunday mornings. The Robin Hood Tea Room opened around 1910 in Kent, Ohio, about the same time as the state normal school (later Kent State University) was begun. It was located directly across the street from campus, as was the Idle Inn in Montgomery, Alabama, opposite the Woman's College. The Davis Tea Room opposite Jesse Hall in Columbia was where University of Missouri students went for daytime "jelly dates" in the 1920s.

Students at Iowa State University could go to the Maples, opened in 1922 by the widow of a professor and later operated by the Home Economics Department. The Edgehill Tea Garden, located in a bungalow on Thirteenth Street, was only one-half block from the University of Utah in Salt Lake City. Meals were served in the garden, where individual lemon-chiffon pies were popular treats. The Wayside Tea Room in Canton, New York, catered to students at St. Lawrence University. University of Chicago students patronized the Studio Tea Shop on East Fifty-seventh, while the Anna Lyon Tea Shop up the street was known to be a "hangout of writers and intellectuals." Students at Columbia University went to King's College Inn, run by Meta S. Young in 1931.

Women's colleges were especially likely to attract tea rooms. The Cottage Tea Room was a favorite of Bryn Mawr girls in 1917, while the Ingelneuk Tea House in Swarthmore, Pennsylvania, was well liked by Swarthmore students. Cherry and orange fritters were popular menu items. In South Hadley, Massachusetts, Mount Holyoke students enjoyed the proximity of the Croysdale Inn, begun in 1909, and expanded when Frances and Isabella Parfitt's brother Jack built them the large stucco building near the college known familiarly as The House That Jack Built. The Co-Z-T Shoppe also operated near Mount Holyoke, as did the Lilacs, halfway between the college and Amherst.

Northampton, Massachusetts, home to Smith College, may have been the queen of college towns when it came to tea shops. At one point in the mid-1920s, the small town of Northampton had about fifteen. Among them were the Arm Chair, the Cedar Stump, the Copper Kettle, the Dutch Oven, the Elms Tea Room, the Home Craft Shop, the Lonesome Pine, Mary Marguerite, Mother's Cupboard, the Plymouth Inn Tea Room, Ye Rose Tree Inn, and the Venture Inn Tea Room.

Flora Castle's Copper Kettle Tea Room on State Street was the first, possibly inspired by the opening of Katherine McClellan's photographic studio on the street in 1905. By 1911, the Rose Tree Inn was creating a sensation on Bridge Street, run by the eccentric Madame Anna de Naucaze, who wore masculine-looking suits. "All Smith is crazy over the Rose Tree Inn," wrote a student to her mother in 1912. She found the food and the dark, candlelit interior wonderful, but the real fascination was with the proprietor. "There is a mystery surrounding her," she wrote. "No one knows whether it is a man or woman." Madame de Naucaze closed her doors in 1923 after Smith College, which regulated students' off-campus activities, removed her from the approved list, saying she had allowed students to smoke.

In 1920 the famed Mary Marguerite opened, the longest-lasting of Northampton's tea rooms, occupying the same location as the Copper Kettle before it. Original owners Mary W. Wells and Marguerite L. Hawks sold it in 1952, but it persisted into the 1960s. The "Mary Marg"'s 1927 advertisement in a Smith alumnae publication said:

Let's meet at the Tea Room at 21 State
For tea and a sandwich and perhaps some cake.
We'll visit and enjoy our afternoon treat
At the Mary Marguerite we'll have our spree.

TOP: MADAME ANNA DE NAUCAZE AS SHE APPEARED IN AN ADVERTISEMENT IN THE SMITH COLLEGE YEARBOOK OF 1919.
(Smith College Archives, Smith College)

BELOW: HER TEA ROOM, THE ROSE TREE INN, WAS LOCATED IN NORTHAMPTON, MASSACHUSETTS.

"SMITH" you have never owed me anything---I owe you much---that is why we are friends.

Yours gratefully

Ye Rose Tree Inn
Northampton,
1919   Mass.

A de Naucaze

ROSE TREE INN, NORTHAMPTON, MASS.

Schrafft's became a training ground for many women who would go on to open their own tea rooms.

In New York, Schrafft's, like the stately Maillard's on Fifth Avenue, offered its patrons restful, but rather stuffy, clublike interiors in which to consume their tea and light repasts. The 383 Fifth Avenue Schrafft's tea room was done in Colonial style, as was the mezzanine at 13 West Forty-second Street, while the small tea room at the 20 West Thirty-eighth Street location was Italianate. Many of the Schrafft's stores had classically styled large rooms with high ceilings, huge windows with shirred-silk Roman shades, chandeliers, and molded plaster pilasters and ceiling medallions. Maillard's, whose 1920s patrons were served sandwiches of cream cheese and white cherries in the atmosphere of a lavish upper-class dining room, had been established in the mid-1900s and was associated with a confectionery business.

In California, a very different note was struck by the Pig 'n Whistle chain of informal eateries. The first Pig 'n Whistle was begun in San Francisco in 1910; by the mid-1930s the chain had eighteen locations in Oakland, Los Angeles, Hollywood, and Pasadena. It did its own baking and made its own ice cream and candy. While it catered afternoon teas, it also had a soda fountain and tried to appeal to the widest possible clientele. Townsend's, in San Francisco and Los Angeles, was similar. From 3 to 5 P.M. it served afternoon tea at its Powell Street location, where melted cream cheese on toast and tea cost 30¢. Like the Pig 'n Whistle, New England's Puritan Tea Rooms and Candy Shops chain offered the convenience and lively busyness of the drugstore lunch counter. Chains like these took the country by storm in the mid-1920s, sending a shiver up the spine of hotel dining-room managers, who were surrounded by competitors at the same time they were stripped of their lucrative alcohol service. "All of the newcomers, the 'Pig 'n Whistles,' the 'Cat 'n Fiddles,' the 'Lunchettes,' the 'Luncheon-ettes,' the 'Have-A-Bites' and the 'What-Nots,'" observed *The Hotel World* in 1924, "are now successfully bidding for the public favor."

Many city tea rooms, including the chains, had grown out of or were associated with candy stores and soda fountains. Louis Sherry's new 1929 ground-floor tea room on Madison and Sixty-second Street contained a candy shop, while its French dining room was on the mezzanine. Architect Ely Jacques Kahn designed New York's Broadmoor Pharmacy (circa 1930) with a sleek soda fountain on the street level, and a men's grill and women's tea room facing each other across a green terrazzo foyer on the lower level. Pittsburgh residents were dazzled by the art deco Reymer Brothers Tea Room and Candy Store, built in 1928 in the Clark Building and designed by Lamont Button. Its ground-floor candy shop was decorated with a stylish mural, *The Bon Bon Tree*, painted by Norwood Gilvary, while a grand staircase of black marble led to the huge tea room above, occupying twice the floor space of the candy shop. Loft's and Huyler's were other well-known chains of candy-store tea rooms. In Detroit's fabulous art deco Fisher Building, designed by Albert Kahn in 1928, Huyler's ran the L'Aiglon tea room.

The candy-store/soda-fountain tea rooms were partly a response to Prohibition; with alcohol forbidden, candy, ice cream, and carbonated beverages became popular as substitute gratifications. At the same time,

AT
Plows
—THE GOOD THINGS TO EAT

MENU FROM PLOWS, A HIGH-PRICED CHICAGO TEA ROOM THAT SOLD CANDY AND SODA FOUNTAIN TREATS. IT WENT OUT OF BUSINESS IN JANUARY OF 1923.

(Chicago Historical Society)

that decade witnessed a reorganization of the candy industry, which stimulated the creation of tea rooms. Whereas much candy had previously been produced by small-time makers and sold in their own shops, national manufacturers selling wrapped and branded candy bars took over in the 1920s, threatening the livelihood of small producers, many of them women or Greek-American men.

Some small candy stores responded by devoting part of their floor space to tea rooms. As a restaurant trade magazine noted in 1924, "A certain confectionery store in Chicago suddenly condensed the candy department to a few square feet of space, put in tables and chairs, and is feeding some 600 working girls a day." It was not alone. Josephine B. Dowd inherited the Betsy Ross Candy Shop in Indianapolis, Indiana, and turned it into a tea room. In 1928 the shop had three soda fountains, one in the tea room, one in the ballroom, and one in a large bowling alley below. Wilhelmina Anne Maxwell backed into the tea room business via a candy store in Missouri. For fifteen years she had been a department store buyer, then she added a few tea tables in her brother's Joplin candy shop. When the tea room prospered, she left her job to run it full-time. Laona Kuhn inherited a candy business from her father and in 1929 turned it into a tea room, Kuhn's, on Woodward Avenue in Detroit. On the first floor she ran a soda fountain and quick service, and on the mezzanine and second floors were the tea rooms proper, while on the third floor she manufactured candy.

Other tea rooms with candy stores (or candy stores with tea rooms) included the Pullman Tea Room on Chapel Street in New Haven, Connecticut, which packaged candies such as its Pantaze bonbons; the tea room on the second floor of the Pulakos Candy Store in Erie, Pennsylvania; the Evangeline Tea and Candy Shoppe, in Lawrence, Massachusetts; and the Copper Kettle Candy Shoppe, Tea Room, and Restaurant on College Avenue in Appleton, Wisconsin. Ethel M. Reickert's Tea Room on Delaware Avenue in Buffalo, New York, occupied nearly an entire building. The large downstairs space served as an ice cream and candy shop, while the tea room was upstairs. In Boston, Murray's Luncheon and Tea Room on Boylston Street sold French *bonbonnières*, fancy ices, and cakes. In San Francisco, the George Haas & Sons Candy Store in the Phelan Building on O'Farrell Street advertised a second-floor tea room decorated in "restful tones of Old Ivory and Wedgewood Blue." The venerable I. Teall Catering Company of Rochester, New York, established in the nineteenth century, ran a tea room and candy store in its three-story building on East Avenue, which also held a ballroom on the second floor and an eleven-room apartment on the third floor.

The Magic of Toast

As tame as the American diet was throughout the first half of the twentieth century, tea rooms managed to be in the vanguard of dietary change. This was largely due to women's concern with nutrition, a subject the male restaurateur (who had far less formal education than most women who ran tea rooms) generally found puzzling. In practice this meant that tea rooms led the way in introducing meals that were light, well-balanced, and contained less meat and more raw and cooked vegetables. Salads had a much more prominent place on tea room menus than in many other eating places. Even in 1928 some big hotels in Chicago had no salads on their menus. One menu listed a meal of cream soup, several heavy meat and bean entrées, potatoes, pastry, coffee, and rolls, reported a restaurateur. Tea rooms also tended to be hygienic. Food critic M.F.K. Fisher said that although their meals were high in calories, tea rooms were dietetically safe because they had no steam tables with béchamel sauce and "iridescent corned beef" (she also enjoyed the absence of juke-boxes).

With its English culinary influences and Northern-tradition dairy-products base, tea room food was not appealing to all Americans, nor was it "just like home" for those whose roots were in Southern or Eastern Europe. There were those, like novelist Edna Ferber, who found the tea room's offerings too bland. "Its fare was of the lettuce-leaf, chopped-apple, marshmallow or cream-sauce school, too anaemic for my Jewish palate, trained to a richer tangier taste," she said.

In the 1920s many Americans acquired new dietary habits, possibly influenced by Prohibition and responses to wartime shortages. Whatever the cause, observers noted the increased consumption of fruits and fruit juices, vegetable dinners, dairy products, specialty breads, toasted sandwiches, French toast, waffles, malted milk, ginger ale, eggs, bacon, ham, poultry, fish, fruit and chicken salads, nuts and cereals, gelatin desserts, soups, and sweet desserts of all kinds. Most of these foods were

THE LADY BALTIMORE CAKE, A WHITE CAKE WITH WHITE FROSTING AND FILLED WITH CHOPPED PECANS, FIGS, DATES, AND RAISINS, WAS A TEA ROOM FAVORITE.

prominent on tea room menus, as were lighter meals. In a *Restaurant Management* article in 1930, "Folks Don't Want Heavy or Fancy Food or Those Disguised by a French Name," a dietitian recommended a bridge luncheon menu typical of a tea room menu, consisting of an orange and mint cup, creamed chicken served in popover shell with green peas, cranberry jelly served on lettuce, nut muffins, and apple gingerbread.

Although they served a lot of sandwiches and pork chops—and even a frankfurter here and there—the magic words on tea room menus were

TEA AT THE BLUE LANTERN INN

salad, homemade, dessert, toast, creamed, stuffed, and *chicken.* Typical hot tea-room entrées included creamed chicken (or creamed eggs, shrimp and peas, celery, pimiento strips, or crabmeat) on waffles or toast, chicken pie, croquettes of all kinds, poached egg on spinach, stuffed green peppers, and omelettes. Entrées were dishes beloved by tea room operators because they could be made up in advance and were thus quick to serve—*and* they used up leftovers. Commonly known as "made dishes," they were more economical than roasts, steaks, or chops. Alice Foote MacDougall grew positively ecstatic when she described the varied uses of leftover turkey, which included "hash, or 'minced and creamed *au gratin en bordure de pommes de terre,*' which grand-sounding name means that your left-over turkey, with a food cost of almost nothing, has become a delicious entrée. Nor is your turkey then exhausted. Still small bits may be found which, mixed with mayonnaise, form a delicious filling for tea sandwiches before you finally consign the carcass to your soup kettle."

Although they often featured dishes whose ingredients were minced and formed into French-influenced timbales, croquettes, croustades, and aspics, by and large tea rooms favored Northern and Southern American home cooking in the English tradition over continental cuisine. Alice MacDougall was typical of tea room owners in her dislike of the standard "continental" restaurant fare of the 1920s. "Sauce Piquante, what culinary crimes have you not camouflaged?" she asked dramatically in her 1935 cookbook. "Salmi of Duck was my pet aversion," she wrote. "Who does not remember that abomination of legs and wings, served up with a sauce in which floated waifs and strays of the olive keg and over which, like flowers at a funeral, nested a few sprigs of weary parsley? Not on my table does Salmi of Duck appear." Indeed, her coffeehouses had regulation tea room cuisine as demonstrated by a September 1928 menu, which featured dishes such as chicken and vegetables in aspic and a salad of pineapple, orange, and white grapes, with a teatime special of a shrimp salad sandwich and toasted wafers Parmesan.

Toast was to the tea room as the french fry is to the hamburger joint. Mere bread simply wouldn't do. The club sandwich owed its popularity to its being on toast, said an article in a restaurant magazine in 1926, with the toast supplying the "friendly touch" the sandwich needed. Creamed dishes were served on toast or waffles. For afternoon tea, cinnamon toast was the most popular choice, and "tea and toast and atmosphere" nicely summed up the essence of the tea room, according to a 1920s poem. Real tea houses were those that served "real toast" that was "thick, soft, and crusty," said a fussy critic. Other forms of bread were also keys to success, and tea rooms may have been the first eating places to make specialties of the bread and rolls they served with meals. The Tick Tock in Hollywood was known for its sticky orange rolls, and popovers were the carefully chosen trademark of Patricia Murphy's Candlelight dining rooms. "I went through lists of hot breads, knowing that hot bread was an item that people who were dining out were not likely to have at home," she said. At Polly's Tea Room in Branford, Connecticut, nut bread was a speciality, while many tea rooms offered cheese bread, gingerbread, orange bread, or brown bread. The Satsuma featured a Southern favorite, spoon bread.

Salads, called "the thinking woman's luncheon, and the university girl's dessert," were also popular attractions in tea rooms. Salad did not typically mean greens until after the Second World War, when the California custom spread across the nation. Ann Heyneman's in San Francisco in 1937 offered a salad of chicory, baby lettuce, escarole, romaine and watercress, dressed with olive oil and vinegar, and topped with chopped chicken livers, hard-boiled egg, and Roquefort cheese—but this was still unusual. Polly's in Los Angeles offered a variety of fruit salads, including grapefruit, avocado, pear, and pineapple. In 1927 the Old Vanity Fair Tea

Room in the Women's Athletic Club of Los Angeles served a Lexington Salad of chopped pineapple, cabbage, peanuts, and green peppers as well as a Shanghai Salad of pineapple, litchi nuts, and fresh raspberries. In most tea rooms outside California, however, salad most often meant a meat, fish, or vegetable concoction, usually prepared with liberal amounts of mayonnaise. At the Community Kitchen in Evanston, Illinois, patrons could order an Italian salad consisting of pasta with peas, pimientos, and—of course—mayonnaise. Pickles were considered the working girl's salad, and the proprietor of the Candy Box on State Street in Chicago said in 1935 that her patrons could not get enough of them.

Boiled down to essentials, tea rooms purveyed a dainty version of homey comfort food prepared by cooks, not chefs. Most took pride in cooking from scratch, using fresh ingredients, and keeping their kitchens clean. Only a few offered adventurous dishes. One proprietor introduced chickpeas to tea room patrons, and in 1920 the Torch of Hawaii in New York served curry made with garlic, cumin, and curry powder. Many, however, were more likely to heed the advice of a 1911 book, *Bright Ideas for Money Making*. The author suggested that a tea room might adopt a Japanese theme with lanterns, paper parasols, and waitresses in kimonos. Rice could be served, she said, "but do not carry the idea of Japanese cooking any further, as there are very few Japanese dishes which are popular." Even big-city tea rooms stuck with plain food that was familiar to middle class, Protestant Americans. One of the most popular items on the menu of San Francisco's Mayflower in the late 1920s was deviled eggs. The 1920 menu at Chicago's Miss Ellis included corned beef hash on toast. Schrafft's featured noodles with giblet sauce in 1931. The Blue Parrot Inn in Denver offered a bowl of bread and milk on their 1935 menu. Mary Lee's had a 35¢ special luncheon on Saturday, January 14, in 1939: frankfurters and sauerkraut, boiled potatoes, roll and butter, and dessert.

"The only thing which doesn't seem to count in a tea-room is tea," said tea lover Agnes Repplier in *To Think of Tea!* in 1932. She noted that American magazine articles on tea rooms rarely referred to the beverage, paying much more attention to color schemes and curtain fabrics. If ever tea was mentioned, she said, it was only when the writer made "the satanic suggestion" to add a piece of preserved ginger or a couple of cloves to the teapot. Writer and Village romeo Max Bodenheim said tea in Greenwich Village was "as rare as a virgin." Everywhere tea drinkers complained of how poorly the beverage was prepared. It was often brewed in tepid water, or tasting of a rusty metal pot. Huge variation in the amount of tea added to a pot was overcome when cheesecloth tea bags became universal in the mid-1930s, after correction of an earlier problem in which the cloth's sizing dissolved in hot water. Most tea rooms offered few types of tea, the usual choice being orange pekoe, or simply "tea." A few menus had a slightly expanded list, with Ceylon and oolong at the Oakford Tea Room in St. Joseph, Missouri, in 1935. The Grace Dodge Hotel for women, in Washington, D.C., perhaps took tea a bit more seriously than most. It had a separate tea house on its property and in the early 1920s served Ceylon, oolong, orange pekoe, English breakfast, mixed, or green teas.

Can a Tea-Man Be a He-Man?

With their emphasis on home cooking, tea rooms should have been popular with men. But the majority of men perceived an abundance of gender signals that kept them away from tea rooms or made them reluctant to admit to liking them. Just as "real men" asserted in the 1970s that they did not eat quiche, their fathers and grandfathers did not eat in tea rooms in the 1920s and 1930s. Most male complaints about tea rooms focused on their "canary bird food" served in "doll-sized portions," but this was only part of the problem.

A number of culinary experts became convinced that men and women liked entirely different foods, and a miniature industry delving into men's likes and dislikes evolved. Men, they said, preferred red meat, pie, and coffee. Miss Farmer's School developed a "Meal for Men" starting off with a sauerkraut-and-tomato-juice cocktail, followed by roast pork, sweet potatoes, wax beans with Bermuda onions, and ice cream pie. The "Ladies Luncheon" featured peanut butter rolls accompanying an avocado cocktail, stuffed lobster, potatoes laurette, dandelion timbales, and a tomato-and-endive salad. One tea room proprietor reported in 1934, "The conventional woman's taste runs to chicken patties, peas, and ice cream; men like steaks, French fried potatoes, and apple pie." Others recommended man-pleasing menu items such as split pea soup, oyster stew, rye bread, and thick meat sandwiches with gravy. Good menu terms for men included *deep-dish, au gratin, fried, broiled, hot, beef, pork,* and *bacon.* The Little Tea Shop was a favorite of businessmen in Memphis, Tennessee, in 1948. Especially popular was its Lacey Special of sliced chicken between halves of corn sticks, all smothered in gravy. Hearty menu choices and big portions were important, but some who examined reasons for men's discomfort with tea rooms decided that the issue was not food, but turf.

Clearly some tea rooms, particularly before the mid-1920s, aimed to appeal to women, and women only. At Gertrude Hastings's tea room, men were "not specifically barred, but a decidedly feminine atmosphere pervades the whole place, which makes a man feel about as much at home as he would feel in a sewing circle," observed *The American Restaurant* in 1920. Aimee Smutz, manager of a Seattle tea room in 1923, was said to believe "not only in votes for women, but food for women." She told a reporter that because she admitted no male patrons, her meals could be delicate and attractive, "far from the barbecue sort of thing." Vera Megowen's places in Evanston were so attuned to women's needs that they provided a compartment under each place at the table to hold a purse.

The mere fact that the majority of patrons were female, however, was probably the main factor that put men off tea rooms. Some men were averse to being in a room filled with women. The comfortable unself-conscious-ness of a man in a man's world disappeared when he entered a women's restaurant, and he became tensely focused on his bodily movements and table manners. About 90 percent of the patrons of the two Clover Coffee Shops in Cleveland, Ohio, were women. This frustrated the proprietor, who repeatedly attempted to win men's business. When the ban on serving beer was lifted in 1933, he became more determined. He put up a notice in one shop saying Gentlemen Exclusively and plastered the walls with bold signs giving the prices of such men's favorites as pig's knuckles, sauerkraut, chili, goulash, and pie à la mode. The strategy worked. One customer, however, still felt a need to drop this note in the comments box: "Women take too long to order. They chatter too much. Keep them out of men's shop." Some tea rooms set aside a separate room and dubbed it a grill room. In most respects grill rooms were identical to tea rooms, although they may have had a bit more dark wood paneling. At

THE 1935 MENU OF DENVER'S BLUE PARROT INN REASSURED MEN THAT THEY WERE WELCOME. PROBABLE "MEN'S CHOICES" ON THIS MENU INCLUDED COLORADO MOUNTAIN TROUT, LEG OF LAMB, STEAK, AND ROAST SQUAB.

the Broadmoor Pharmacy in New York, the same furniture and flooring were used in both the tea room and the grill room across the hallway. The tea room, however, was "light and gay," with mirrored pillars and glass-topped tables, while the grill room was all in walnut. Typically grill rooms differed significantly from tea rooms in one critical respect: they barred women.

Tea rooms that wanted to expand their patronage, especially in the Depression, came to realize they had to make men feel comfortable. Dropping *tea room* from their name or changing it to *coffee shop* was a common tactic. Mabel Orgelman, who ran the Green Lantern Tea Room in Providence, Rhode Island, in 1922, changed the name to the Green Lantern after her place was discovered by a group of advertising men, to ensure it would remain a popular place for men's business banquets. Many tea rooms called themselves coffee shops from the start. The connotations of *coffee* were clear enough. As enunciated by a hotel journal in 1923: "Tea Room suggests dainty eating; Coffee Room suggest hearty eating." Having good coffee was also seen as important to men, and many tea rooms made a point of advertising their coffee. One tea room proprietor said she searched for months for a "man's coffee."

Tea rooms realized what they most needed to change were men's perceptions, and the way to do it was to change the signals they sent. For the most part, male patronage could be won through small changes. Among things men disliked in tea rooms, said the experts, were candles, women smoking, round tables, wrapped sugar cubes (men did not know what to do with the wrappings), paper doilies whose edges curled, antique china, and tiny salt and pepper shakers. Restaurant consultant Joseph Dahl implored tea rooms to provide "lintless" napkins that wouldn't shed on dark business suits.

Despite all the hazards, many men did patronize tea rooms, all the while publicly disavowing them. *The Restaurant and Tea Room Journal* claimed, somewhat dubiously, in 1925, "Masculine Trade Forms Bulk of Patronage" in metropolitan tea rooms. While this assertion was unconvincing, tea rooms were popular places for male business gatherings. University of Missouri alumni met weekly at the Busy Bee Tea Room in St. Louis in 1929, while the Kiwanis Club of Los Gatos, California, met at the Black Cat Tea Room on South Santa Cruz Avenue in 1933. The Rotary Club met at the Doll House Tea Room in Lakewood, New Jersey, in 1940, and the American Astronomical Society held its annual convention dinner at Vera Megowen's in Evanston in 1942. The Christopher House Tea Room in Freehold, New Jersey, drew more male patrons than women in 1937, many of them judges and lawyers from the courthouse.

Duncan Hines, a restaurant guidebook writer of the 1930s and 1940s who believed that two-thirds of American eateries were so bad they should be "padlocked," often recommended tea rooms as the best places to eat. When he was interviewed in 1941, he told his male interviewer (who admitted to "spinning-wheel trouble") that if he would "brave the whimsy," he would discover fine home cooking in tea rooms. Frequently, though, Hines enclosed his positive comments in a set of gendered parentheses. In 1937, for instance, he reported that a local man said of the Casco Bay Tea Room in Yarmouth, Maine: "Don't be scared of the name tea room." Hines often took the presence of men in a tea room as proof of its quality. As he said of the Vassar House in 1937, "Men like it, always a sign that the food is all right."

Hines was one of several guidebook authors who tried to bolster masculine confidence on the subject of tea rooms. John Drury (*Dining in Chicago*, 1931) said of the Vassar House (which had a men's grill), "Fully seventy-five per cent of its clientele is made up of real honest-to-goodness he men." One of the books most acidly conditional in its praise of tea rooms was the 1934 New York restaurant guide *Tips on Tables*. It said of Susan Palmer's, "It has all the lavender and lace earmarks of a tea-room upstairs, but there's a subterranean oyster bar and grill...made all for comfort." When Alice Foote MacDougall's Firenze changed hands in 1933, *Tips on Tables* said it had become "an establishment for people who wine and dine, instead of for people who sip." Of Anne Miller's on West Eighth: "Men dine here unabashedly and overlook the doilies." The book emphasized that Mary Elizabeth's was not a New England–style tea room, "lest the curse be put upon it at the start."

❖ ❖ ❖

If men found the average city tea room challenging, this went double for the flamboyant exercises in imagination represented by fortune-telling "Gypsy" tea rooms and other places out of the mainstream. However annoying they found delicate dishes and doilies, feminine whimsy was even harder to handle. Women, of course, ate it up. Gypsy tea rooms and the other offbeat tea rooms that developed in the late 1920s and 1930s carried on the Greenwich Village tradition of seeking fun with meals.

CHAPTER SIX

Outrageously Orange

The success of a tea room is dependent not only upon the quality of the food served,
but also upon the way it plays upon the imagination of its guests.

—*TEA ROOM AND GIFT SHOP*, AUGUST 1923

he fortune-telling "Gypsy" tea rooms that proliferated in the late 1920s and the 1930s, along with zanily colorful little shops, Russian tea rooms, and places decorated to resemble quaint Italian piazzas, provided entertainment and escape for their patrons and drew from a wider social-class spectrum than any other sorts of tea room.

During the Depression, *American Cookery* observed, "Girls who have no charm or beauty in their homes or lives at all frequent these tea rooms to enjoy their atmosphere." By the mid-1930s, according to the article, when a woman heard the words *tea room*, she thought of "cozy little places with dimmed lights and candles; walls and furniture glaring in red; weird, fantastic colorings—a place where she may invite a friend or a girl chum, have a dainty luncheon, and gossip."

It almost seemed that as women tried to escape their homes—in tea rooms that were as unlike home as possible—men looked for eating places that were home replacements. The Richards-Treat in Minneapolis, one of a handful of tea rooms with cafeteria service, said men were very responsive to the restful decor and homelike atmosphere projected by their dark green tables and chairs, curly-maple cupboard filled with blue willowware and Wedgwood, hand-colored prints, and mahogany mirrors. Alice Foote MacDougall kept one foot in each camp, avoiding the "deadly" standardization of hotel dining rooms, on the one hand, and digestion-destroying "cubistic and ultramodern" decor on the other. She offered her romance-seeking diners the illusion of being in Italian or Spanish courtyards, yet kept noise levels down, lights dim, and colors subdued for those comfort seekers who needed to unwind. She wanted men, who were likely to fall in the latter category, to feel at home in her restaurants.

As early as the late teens, the idea that tea rooms were eating places uniquely characterized by "atmosphere" had become a doctrine. Tea rooms were in stark contrast with the majority of eating places, whose bare interiors, at their best, were expressive of cleanliness. Tea room atmosphere could clearly be either of two radically different varieties—cultured refinement or fun—with fun gaining ground after Greenwich Village became famous. By the late 1920s, the restaurant industry as a whole was convinced that eating places had to provide a jolly atmosphere. Restaurants and lunchrooms removed wood paneling or stripped off hygenic white tiles and added color, wall decorations, and interesting lamps. Even the plain-Jane cafeteria jumped on the bandwagon. In November of 1928 a story in *Cafeteria Management* proclaimed "The Era of 'Atmosphere' is Now Here." By emulating the tea room, the story said, the cafeteria could "please the public demand for the unique," a demand that would only grow stronger with the economic collapse of 1929.

Color Crazy

Americans, women in particular, fell in love with color in the 1920s. Suddenly everything that had been black, white, or drab became colorful, from cars to clothing, umbrellas, draperies, and even radiators. Women rejected architect-approved blue and white kitchens, opting instead for apricot, peach, persimmon, and apple-green walls, floors, and cabinets. The all-white bathroom also looked outmoded and cried out for colorful accessories. Up-to-date brides chose wedding cake "no longer coldly snowy, but...decorated with garlands in pastel tints," according to a 1927 magazine.

Bright colors, popularized in Greenwich Village's "loudly colored caverns with fantastic names," conveyed a spirit of youthful joie de vivre. In the Village, painters inspired by the European art movements fauvism and futurism had returned to New York in 1914 and splashed color "joyously over everything in sight." Red, yellow, and purple were popular colors, but orange was tops. The Candlestick, near Washington Square, was one of the many Village tea shops that chose orange for its color scheme. Known for its "vegetables and poetesses," it combined orange with blue in 1916.

The popularity of orange soon spread way beyond lower Manhattan. The Orange and Black Tea Room operated on West Forty-ninth Street in 1918. The Lilacs in South Hadley, Massachusetts, chose orange for its chairs in 1920, while Nantucket's Skipper used orange and green for its furniture and striped awnings. Surprisingly, the city fathers approved the Skipper's orange lamppost outside holding its sign. The Maramor in Columbus, Ohio, picked orange for the tabletops in its second-floor party room, and the Pine Tree Tea Room in Rochester, New York, redecorated in 1924, adopted a color scheme of orange, black, turquoise, and gray. In 1924, an architecture journal gave its approval, telling its readers that while red was a satisfying color, and yellow was interesting, orange (which combined red and yellow) was "the most satisfying and interest-ing of all."

Other bright colors were popular too. At the Drowsy Saint Inn, in Croton-on-Hudson, Jane Burr furnished with Colonial furniture the rooms she rented to writers, but decorated her tea room with gay colors in Greenwich Village style. Yellow and black was a well-liked combination in Greenwich Village and beyond. The Pierrette Tea Shop on New York's South William Street painted the outside of its building, formerly a liquor warehouse, in these colors. Inside were black glass-topped tables, yellow curtains with black ribbons, and Pierrette and Pierrot silhouettes in black. The Twin Oaks Coffee Mill, north of Worcester, Massachusetts, combined yellow chairs with black tables.

Red, which psychologists said loosened inhibitions, was dubbed "the spending color" in the 1920s. As a result, earnest and conservative tea room adviser Ralph Elliott recommended that tea rooms (which he believed should be homelike) stay away from this color. It should only be used in places that combined meals with entertainment or dancing, he said. Despite his advice, red remained popular. The Bancroft House in Springfield, Ohio, underwent a Cinderella-like transformation each day in the early 1920s. After lunch the sober white tablecloths were stripped off, revealing bright red tabletops. The walls were hung with tapestries, birdcages with live birds were suspended from the ceiling, and a society woman came in to preside over the festivities. After teatime, everything was removed, the white tablecloths were restored, and dinner was served. The Hotel Savery in Des Moines, Iowa, chose red and black lacquer for its Chinese-theme tea room, dressing its waitresses in Chinese costumes.

Many tea rooms explored "the limitless possibilities in a pot of paint," adopting the multicolor look so popular in the 1920s. Some places painted plain tables and chairs, and sometimes even antiques, all in different mix-and-match colors. One tea room had tables of vermilion, amber, crimson, primrose yellow, cerulean blue, and emerald green, with goblets and dishes matching the color of the tables they were used on. In 1923, the Tintern Tea Garden in Washington, D.C., painted its pine tables black and the chairs in various colors such as orange, lavender, and crimson. The parrot became the symbol of multicolorism in tea room interiors and tea room names as well. Tea rooms named for blue, green, red, and black (perhaps in protest?) parrots dotted the land; parrot motifs spread like wildfire. Nan's Kitchen in Boston painted parrots on the sides of its wooden booths. The Orpheum Tea Room, which opened in Wichita, Kansas, in 1923 painted Egyptian parrots on the walls and on their china plates. The Skipper used curtain fabric decorated with large parrots in vivid greens, blues, reds, and yellows.

Color dominated tea room names, with blue in the lead, followed by green. Blue Bird was so often used as a tea room name that it was declared "stale" in 1932. Beyond birds and parrots, Blue was also combined with Tea Pot (Chicago and Salem, Indiana), Horse (Greenwich Village), Paradise (Greenwich Village), Lantern (Philadelphia, Louisville, Kentucky, and New Preston, Connecticut), Moon (Syracuse, New York, and Westerly, Rhode Island), Dragon (Barre, Massachusetts), Bell (Saratoga Springs, New York), Bowl (Wilmington, New York, and New York City), Pitcher (Brockport, New York), Plate (New York City and West Hartford, Connecticut), Mill (Washington, D.C.), Door (Chester, Massachusetts, and East Orange, New Jersey), Grass (Miami), Ship (Boston), Mouse (Chicago), Dog (Provincetown), Heron (Newcastle, Maine), Anchor (Newbury, Massachusetts), Mushroom (Greenwich Village), Candle (Danielson, Connecticut), and Gables (Fayetteville, Arkansas). Green combined with many of the above, as well as Arbor, Witch, Apple, Gate, Kettle, Shutters, Barn, Shingle, Pump, and Meadow.

Every aspect of tea rooms was invaded by color. The ever-conservative Lewis Tea Room Institute ("neutral walls are a safe selection") suggested a color scheme of cobalt blue and yellow that "may be carried out in gingham drapes, uniforms for waitresses, even in wrapping paper and twine for packages." For the timid they advocated using bowls of bright red apples, oranges, or grapefruit to "make brilliant spots of color against dull walls." Many tea rooms used colorful glass dishes or imported peasant pottery. "Tea Room," a poem of the early 1920s, described a possible color palette like this:

Of course the dishes are not mates:

The cups are yellow, and the plates

Are green like grass; cut lemons gleam

On lacquer red; the yellow cream

Is in a black jug, squat and droll;

The sugar in an orange bowl.

Hostess and waitress uniforms were issued in a range of colors like jade green, ciel blue, and champagne. "The vogue for color is more pronounced this year than ever," announced the Angelica uniform catalog of 1929. To enliven a white uniform it offered "apronettes" in nine colors. In this riotous context, a tea room without color sent a message that it was "refined." At the dignified Moseley Tea Room in New York City, for instance, manager Romona Swainey dressed her waitresses in traditional black dresses with white aprons with large scallops at the side and on the caps. (Rejecting gaudiness, its brown-walled interior was furnished with subdued mahogany furniture and black-topped tables.)

Food did not escape the attention of the tea room colorist. An avocado-and-cream-cheese tea sandwich might seem more colorful if named a "jade and ivory" sandwich. Candlelight's Patricia Murphy said she always paid attention to color contrasts in food. "There is no excuse for heaping a plate with dull brown and white edibles, all tasting very much alike," she said. Garnishes of pickle or cress helped dress up a plate of sandwiches, as did a flower, a recommendation of cooking teacher Alice Bradley. The Lewis Tea Room Institute pointed out that while green parsley, red tomato, and yellow lemon were all excellent garnishes, "butter and sugar may be colored to make any desired color."

Just like the Movies

Taking a lesson from the tea room—which he believed had a truly cozy atmosphere—restaurant consultant Joseph Dahl recommended in 1927 that restaurants give their patrons "Romance!" He suggested that an old-world street in Spain or Italy could be so cleverly reproduced that "the thrills derived are little less than from the real thing." The grill room of the Benjamin Franklin Hotel in Philadelphia was his idea of a success story. In 1927 it tore out its wood paneling and built a village courtyard surrounded by vine-covered, stuccoed walls and red-tile rooftops, a decorating style found in numerous tea rooms of the decade.

What inspired the profusion of Old World courtyard interiors in tea rooms in the 1920s is unclear, although Spanish-revival styles were also becoming popular in home interiors then. Hollywood films portraying exotic locations undoubtedly stimulated a fascination with unusual interiors. One of the early "scenographic" tea rooms was the Allies' Shop in St. Louis, designed to look like a village in Normandy, France, and run to benefit the American Fund for French Wounded in World War I. Architect Guy Study and a team of artists created the shop's sturdy ("not papier-mâché") interior out of thatched-roof cottages and the ruins of a thirteenth-century church, with realistic touches like a wall topped with broken bottles. Apple-green tables and chairs "spread fête-like into the street," while the "twilight feeling of late afternoon" filtered weakly from wrought-iron lanterns, according to *American Architect* in 1919. Miller's English Tea Room in Fort Wayne, Indiana, adopted an English theme, with columns that imitated ancient oak trees, a flagstone floor, and half-timbered cottage fronts.

Alice Foote MacDougall's Italian and Spanish courtyard interiors—which despite their differing national origins greatly resembled each other—were often imitated. The vogue for Spanish-village interiors was unstoppable in the 1920s. With a perplexing name, the Betsy Ross Tea Room in Indianapolis nonetheless presented its visitors with a Spanish-style interior complete with rough plaster walls, red-tile roofs, bronze lanterns, and Moorish grillwork. In like vein, the Normandy in Chicago inexplicably had a "Spanish Court in No Man's Land." The Lyric Spanish Tea Room in Endicott, New York, at least kept its theme consistent with its name, with deep stucco alcoves along two walls and a painting of a flamenco dancer occupying a focal point at the end of the room. Sherry's Tea Room in Cooperstown, New York, had patrons pass through archways to reach their booths. Like many another Spanish-village tea room, Sherry's artfully draped a colorful shawl from an iron balcony set into its stuccoed, tile-roofed walls. The profusely decorated Seville Café in Rochester, Minnesota, draped Oriental carpets from what appeared to be a clothesline and filled mini-balconies with potted palms. The Casa de Alhambra in Naperville, Illinois, merely hinted at the Moorish with an archway, a bit of grillwork, and two hanging crossed swords. MacDonald's Tea Room in Salem, Massachusetts, boldly departed from the town's witch theme, re-creating a courtyard scene with the usual stucco and arches, adding a "weather-beaten" door with wrought-iron hardware at the rear of the soda-fountain/candy-store tea shop.

In St. Louis, Elsa Conrad's Castilla interpreted Alice Foote Mac-Dougall's decor faithfully, blending elements from both MacDougall's Cortile and Sevillia. Conrad, who "transformed a grim-looking, dingy store into a castle," began her restaurant career with the more pedestrian B&G Sandwich Shop chain. Castilla was filled with every element known to the courtyard genre: draped shawls, wrought-iron window grates,

crumbling stucco walls revealing brick beneath, alcoves, red tiles, vines, and lanterns. Just as at Mac-Dougall's Firenze, waitresses filled copper water jugs from a courtyard well. A booklet about Castilla told how Elsa Conrad had spent hours in the Old World trying to persuade "an uncomprehending peasant to part with an old street lamp" and described the Castilla's treasures, such as a convent bell from the thirteenth century, and a lamp "whose shade was made from the pages of a Spanish bible." In the gift shop patrons could buy tea sets, copper water jugs, and Venetian glass, or order hooked rugs made in Spain.

TOP: SPANISH-VILLAGE INTERIOR OF THE CASTILLA IN ST. LOUIS.

BOTTOM: COVER OF THE 1940 CASTILLA MENU.

Stage-setting in scenographic tea shops was often accompanied by costuming the staff. "Costumes Increase Atmosphere," announced a 1923 story in *Tea Room and Gift Shop*. Waitresses at the Allies Shop wore blue peasant costumes with flaring white organdy headdresses. Alice Foote Mac-Dougall chose light-skinned African-Americans to play Italian *contadiné* in bright head scarves and blousy dresses with full skirts. Elsa Conrad dressed her Castilla waitresses in similar costumes, although in this case they were meant to be Spanish. In New York's Pullman Car Tea Shop, African-American men (male waiters were unusual in tea rooms) dressed as train porters and served guests from tea wagons they rolled down the aisle. Colonial tea rooms often dressed their servers in quaint costumes. The Sunset Tea Room in Connecticut outfitted its waitresses as Dutch girls. Quite a few Chinese-style tea rooms, such as San Francisco's Temple Bar Tea Room on Tillman Place, employed Chinese waitresses dressed in "native costumes."

Tea à la Russe

Russian tea rooms run by refugees from the 1917 revolution proliferated in cities for a time. One of the earliest was in Greenwich Village, in Sheridan Square in 1917. About the same time, a place called the Samovar operated at 6 East Thirty-sixth Street. It was, reputedly, "a new, exclusive and up-to-date tea room" that served Russian tea à la Petrograd. (In its American interpretation in the early 1920s, Russian tea was typically hot tea with a slice of lemon and a maraschino cherry, served in a tall glass with a handle.) Greenwich Village's Samovar, operated by Nanni Bailey, was located at 150 West Fourth Street in 1924 and had dancing starting at 9 P.M. Its not-at-all-Russian menu included New England baked beans and pumpkin pie. A Russian Art Restaurant on the corner of Second Avenue and Twelfth Street operated in 1927. Offering no afternoon tea, and with dancing to a "Balalaika Jazz Orchestra," it does not appear to have been a tea room. The same could be said of many Russian restaurants, including "the" Russian Tea Room on West Fifty-seventh Street next to Carnegie Hall in New York, created in 1932 and established in its well-known configuration in 1946, which was long a celebrity restaurant whose menu included Russian dishes. Its predecessor, however, a small shop located on the opposite side of the street at number 147, may indeed have been a tea room.

Other Russian Tea Rooms and Samovars operated elsewhere in the United States. Around 1920 there was a Russian Tea Room and Peasant Industries (its name was later changed to Russian Tea Room and Art Shop) on South Michigan Boulevard in Chicago. In 1921 Bailey's Samovar was located four miles north of Plymouth, Massachusetts. In 1922 a Samovar Tea Room operated on Sheridan Road in the Chicago area. A Samovar Tea Room and Russian Peasant Handicraft Center was at 35 North Euclid Avenue in Pasadena, California, and a Russian Grill and Tea Room was on the corner of Avery and Tremont in Boston. In Connecticut, the Russian Bear

AT THE RUSSIAN TEA ROOM AND ART SHOP IN CHICAGO, ON THE SECOND FLOOR OF THE LAKE VIEW BUILDING AT 116 SOUTH MICHIGAN BOULEVARD, AFTERNOON TEA WAS SERVED IN TALL GLASSES.

Tea Room was in Thompson, and the Russian Samovar Tea House was located in Coventry. According to Duncan Hines in 1946, the Russian Samovar was run by the Prolesky family, who had escaped the revolution. They printed no menus, but their Russian cook would prepare any exotic dish a customer ordered.

Russian tea rooms were known for their flamboyant interiors and drew a broad clientele. In 1920, sociologist Frances Donovan noted that in Chicago they were patronized extensively by waitresses, especially in their afternoon breaks between lunch and dinner work hours. However, Russian tea rooms were not to the liking of the sometimes-haughty Alice Foote MacDougall, who was offended by their too stimulating interiors. "It may be charity to the Russian refugees to eat in a restaurant where wild splashes of red, yellow, and green dart at you from every corner, but I can't think it very restful," she said in 1928.

Eventually, a Russian tea room became just another style any tea room owner could adopt. As a 1932 tea room correspondence course asked, "Do you want them to feel, upon eating in your place, that it is comfortable, home-like, unusual, exclusive, distinctive, bizarre, attractive, beautiful, Spanish, Italian, or Russian?"

Reading the Tea Leaves

In the late 1920s, a number of tea rooms began to advertise fortune-telling, often by Gypsies. Rom Gypsies had emigrated to the United States from England in the mid-nineteenth century, and from Serbia, Russia, and Austria-Hungary beginning in the 1880s. Fortune-telling was an enterprise often practiced by Rom women in urban areas, but many cities tried their best to restrict it in the early twentieth century. As a consequence fortune-tellers in tea shops often could not charge for their services or be paid by the establishment, but could receive tips directly from customers. Many tea rooms added this attraction to their offerings, and some tea rooms were founded on it, calling themselves Gypsy tea rooms. Probably every major city had at least one Gypsy tea room. Since some Rom Gypsies had been in the confectionery business, it is possible they may sometimes have owned these tea rooms as well. Greenwich Village's Romany Marie (Marchand), probably the nation's best-known "Gypsy," introduced fortune-telling to the Village in her tea room circa 1918. Although she was a native of Moldavia, it is likely she adopted, or at least enhanced, her Gypsy identity for business purposes.

Princess Karina, one of ten fortune-tellers working in a busy tea room, was the American-born daughter of English Gypsies who had immigrated around 1880. She dressed in a colorful getup with lots of jewelry and read about one hundred teacups a day in 1929. The craft was growing in popularity, she said, with more readers plying their trade all the time. She admitted to readers of the *North American Review* that it was not tea leaves but faces, hands, manners, and mannerisms, as well as "many small details of dress and personality," that revealed a person's situation and concerns. The tea leaves, she said, "are not much more than stage properties for a private demonstration of practical psychology." Her tea room clients, who included the young and the old, the rich and the poor, expected nothing more than "mild amusement," but often became engaged by her insights.

Among the specifically Gypsy tea rooms of the 1920s and early 1930s were Elizabeth Trinkner's Gypsy Tea Room in Cleveland, the Gypsy Tea Shop across from the Famous-Barr store in downtown St. Louis, the Gypsy Inn at 200 Fourth Street North in St. Petersburg, Florida, and the Persian Tea Room at 16 West Jackson in Chicago. The Garden of Zanzibar Tea Room, at 54 West Randolph in Chicago, was one of several fortune-telling tea shops that sprang up all over the Loop late in the 1920s. The Gypsy Tea Shop at 22 West Munroe may have been Chicago's first tea room. At the Queen of Hearts Tea Room on North Dearborn, customers could not only have their tea leaves read but also their palms. Forecasting by cards, crystals, and numerology was also available. Pittsburgh had a Gypsy Tea Shop at 207 Fifth Avenue, while Boston's was on the second floor at 160 Tremont, circa 1932. The Gypsy Tea Kettle had numerous locations in New York City. Its original location was at 554 Fifth Avenue, next door to Schrafft's.

Many tea rooms without *Gypsy* in their name also featured tea-leaf reading. At the Iron Gate Inn on N Street in Washington, D.C., which was operated by the Federation of Women's Clubs, a pamphlet announced, "Madame Marie will read your future in the tea leaves, if you wish." New York's Campfire Inn on Fifty-fifth Street offered readings as well. In the 1930s at the Orange Lantern Tea Room, on the third floor of the Central Building in Portland, Oregon, a woman with long black hair told fortunes in a booth with gaily colored curtains. A former student at the University of Oregon and a member of the Unity Church, she was not a Gypsy but she dressed in a long dress, a gingham head scarf, and many bracelets. In 1936, New York City's Vienna Tea Room and Pastry Shop on East Sixtieth Street advertised free tea-leaf or palm readings by Madame Day with checks over 25¢. Evidently Gypsy tea rooms were not known for their cuisine, because the New Vienna announced in boldface on their business card, "Not a 'Gypsy' Place but, Good Food at Regular Prices."

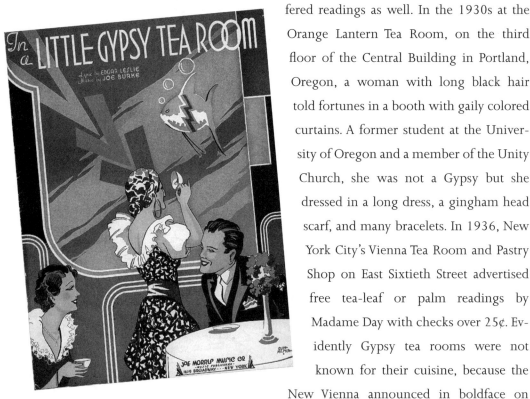

SHEET MUSIC FOR A 1935 SONG ABOUT A MAN WHO HAS HIS HEART "STOLEN AWAY" IN A GYPSY TEA ROOM AFTER HAVING HIS FORTUNE TOLD.

During the Depression, prices fell and many tea rooms advertised free tea-leaf readings to draw customers. Patrons at the Romany Inn, on Sunset Boulevard near Vine in Hollywood, paid only 25¢ for lunch and a reading in 1934. In 1936, the Egyptian Tea Room on Grand Avenue in Kansas City charged 35¢ for lunch and a free teacup reading. Even prices this low were not always enough to attract business, for one patron caught sight of two palmists "solemnly telling one another's fortune with cards" in an Eastern tea room around this time. Fortune-tellers noticed their clients' usual interest in romantic predictions was being temporarily displaced by job-hunting concerns. Customers at the Orange Lantern in Portland, reported the fortune-teller, were looking for employment and hoping that she could tell them where to find it.

Fanciful Food

In an ideal world, a tea room's menu would mirror its concept and its decor, with audacious food matching wild decor and offbeat fun. This was rarely the case. New York's Gypsy Tea Kettle chain had a menu quite similar to that of an F.W. Woolworth lunch counter, with grilled cheese, tuna sandwiches, and other completely ordinary selections. Yet, from time to time, tea rooms came up with some unforgettable items. And in a few cases, tea room concoctions did match the rooms they were consumed in, at least in spirit.

A Petrograd Supreme graced the menu of Chicago's highly decorated Russian Tea Room on South Michigan in 1923. It was an early example of the much later 1990s craze for vertical food: a towering, all-in-one creation that allowed the diner to eat all her courses on a single plate, from top to bottom, appetizer to dessert. St. Louis's Castilla carried its Spanish theme into its menu, at least in part. Alongside the standard American fare of steaks and chicken, Castilla offered a Spanish Dinner for $1.25 in 1938. The names of the dishes were in Spanish, followed by an English translation. Enchaladis [sic] con Frijoles was translated as "A Tasty Spanish meat

"EATING SHOULD BE A FINE ART"

Maybe it was because she hired a publicist in 1921 that Alice Foote MacDougall achieved such fame in the 1920s. Her personal success story, in which her husband falls ill and she must support herself and her three children, was told repeatedly in books and magazines of the 1920s and may have provided the basis for Fannie Hurst's best-seller *Imitation of Life*. According to the legend, MacDougall, possessing just $38, started a business as a New York City coffee dealer in 1907, going from there to open a string of tea-roomy restaurants. At one point in 1928, she (or was it her publicist, trying to make her sound candid?) commented, "How tired I did get of that woman and those interminable three!"

She started her first Little Coffee Shop, in Grand Central Station, around 1921, then opened her romantic courtyard eating places: Cortile, Piazzetta, Firenze, Sevillia, and last, Auberge. Whether Italian, Spanish, or French, all the courtyards were contrived to make visitors feel as if they were sitting outdoors in an old European village square. Wishing to borrow tricks from film and stage sets for her Piazzetta, MacDougall employed set designers who had worked under Norman Bel Geddes on *The Miracle*, a play for which the entire Century Theater was transformed into a Gothic cathedral, all seats replaced with church pews. In the Firenze, she had a scenic artist build a replica of the Ponte Vecchio in Florence. Not surprisingly, the Firenze once served as a movie set itself.

MacDougall was extremely critical of the mainstream American restaurant, condemning it for being boring, noisy, and ugly, and serving mediocre food. Never one to mince words, MacDougall spoke out for aesthetics every chance she got: "When I started business I was forced to eat in restaurants where china, white, thick, and hideous was used." She, by contrast, used delicate dishes in tints of yellow, blue, turquoise, and lilac, with crescent-shaped plates for salads; breakage at Firenze alone cost her over $7,000 in 1927. Among her other dislikes were tables set in rows, "greasy gravy," "the public napkin," and "the deadly monotony of chain-hotel food." To create a restful haven "from the blare of the street" and to feed souls as well as bodies, in the late 1920s she reported burning $10,000 worth of candles for tea and dinner. As she once said, "I'd rather see that little actress crocheting in that corner over her cup of tea than clear a dollar from every customer entering here."

Customers of her coffee and tea business, which she ran with her sons, included tea shops around the country, among them the Tea Chest, in Coconut Grove, and the Flume Reservation Tea House, in New Hampshire, which listed "Alice Foote MacDougall Coffee with Pure Jersey Cream" on its 1935 menu. In correspondence with the Tea Chest in 1922, MacDougall wrote, "I suggest most decidedly that you put in your tea room the three teas which I carry, i.e., Jasmine, Orange Pekoe and Ming Cha," and included advice on how to store tea over the summer.

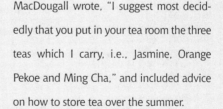

OPPOSITE PAGE: ALICE FOOTE MACDOUGALL; *TOP:* HER FIRST COURTYARD RESTAURANT, THE CORTILE; AND AN ADVERTISEMENT FOR HER COFFEEHOUSES IN A NEW YORK CITY VISITORS' GUIDE OF 1927, WHICH DEPICTS THE FIRENZE.

with Spanish Beans." More memorable, though, was a recipe owner Elsa Conrad said was original to her tea room, Surprise Balls. A marshmallow was put inside a ball of cold mashed sweet potatoes, then rolled in egg and cornflakes and deep-fried.

"Surprise" and "mystery" dishes cropped up again and again on tea room menus, some sounding delicious, others frightful. Schrafft's 1931 menu had an unfortunate-sounding Egg Surprise with Special Dressing. Greenwich Village's Blue Horse delighted in inventing amusing names such as Tomato Surprise, Tomato Caprice, and Tomato Wiggle. Their (non-alcoholic) drinks went a step further, with Pink Goat's Delight and Blue Horse's Neck, each the name of a cocktail from days of old, but with un-expected color added. The Green Arbor Tea House in Concord, Massachu-setts, had both Cheese Dreams and Mystery Cakes on its 1917 menu, the latter named by patrons who failed to guess what was in them. (Cheese dreams, made by spreading cheese, mustard, and cayenne pepper on a bread round and baking it, were tea room staples.)

At the Old Hundred in Connecticut, the filling for a Novelty Sand-wich was made by chopping a small onion, ten pitted olives, one green pepper, and a dill pickle, then mixing it all with cottage cheese. Even Mary Elizabeth's produced a truly odd dish, a peanut butter sandwich with finely chopped stuffed olives, seasoned with lemon juice and Worcester-shire sauce and served on brown bread. Alice Foote MacDougall's restau-rants were known for good food, but her Economy Sandwich, the recipe for which is in her 1935 cookbook, goes overboard in using up leftovers. It is made of cooked peas, string beans, and cauliflower, along with a few radishes and some green pepper. All are to be chopped very fine, mixed with mayonnaise, and spread between thin slices of buttered bread, one white and one whole wheat.

Although Harriet Moody, founder of Chicago's Home Delicacies Association, came as close to providing gourmet food as any tea room proprietor, she too succumbed to the mystery game, with her Queen's Sandwich, made of Brie cheese and honey. "Be careful not to get honey on the edges of the slices of bread," she said, "as the sandwich must not be sticky. These honey and cheese sandwiches puzzle your guests pleasurably."

The 1920s was the decade of the salad, largely because of women's love of this dish, which seemed to lend itself so well to its maker's ingenuity. Often, if it was served in a bowl fitted into a stemmed glass filled with crushed ice, it was called a supreme or cocktail, the former's ingredients being scooped out with a ball cutter, the latter's diced or sliced. Names such as Astoria, Belvedere, Bon Ton, Martini, and Tango were equally fancy and clearly aimed at preserving a little pre-Prohibition glamour. A Martini was not a gin drink but an orange shell filled with peeled grapes, celery, diced apple, chopped walnuts, and mayonnaise. Carr's Catering in Providence, Rhode Island, catered afternoon teas and bridge games on its second floor. Its fancy salads included the Sicilian, the Hawaiian, the Tillinghast, and the inevitable Tomato Surprise. The many Alligator Pear Lorenzos, Cucumber Boats, and Tomato Volgas on menus showed that almost anything could be scooped out and filled with some diced mixture liberally dressed with mayonnaise or French dressing.

Epicurean critics were often appalled at tea room salads. "Atrocities have been committed in the name of the salad," exclaimed a *Restaurant Management* story in 1928. Some thought it was because of a "feminine whimsey for making the eye rule the stomach." Among the fanciful salads patrons encountered in tea rooms was a pineapple salad fashioned to look like a butterfly served at the Brittany in Newark, New Jersey. Under the title "Novel Sandwich Fillings," *Restaurant and Tea Room Journal* presented a

recipe in 1925, though whether sandwich filling or salad, who could know? It contained cottage cheese with marshmallows, chopped raisins, and cherries, with a little salad dressing.

Tea rooms had an inclination to make food resemble something else. At Virginia McDonald's famed tea room in Gallatin, Missouri, she featured salads with special garnishes such as shrimp, tomato, or radish roses, egg sailboats, and cheese strawberries. The sailboats were made of one-half of a hard-boiled egg with a large, three-cornered piece of tuna serving as the sail. Nellie Brown, of Old Hundred, liked Roquefort-cheese carrots, in which Roquefort was mixed with cream cheese, rolled in the shape of a carrot, and covered in cracker crumbs and then in paprika, with a sprig of parsley stuck in the end.

❖ ❖ ❖

Whatever their offenses and limitations, the success of zany tea rooms of the 1920s and 1930s showed that the female sex was bent on having fun, even playing with its food. With plenty of places designed just for them, women no longer had to subordinate their enjoyment or to seek their entertainment exclusively in the home and the church hall.

CHAPTER SEVEN

The Department of Tea

The homelike cuisine, the quiet, efficient service, the refined appointments, appeal especially to those who prefer to lunch without too much diversion.

—WOODWARD & LOTHROP BROCHURE, CIRCA 1930

Department stores were home to some of the longest-lived tea rooms, beginning in the nineteenth century and going strong until the 1960s, with a few surviving today. These tea rooms, more than any other kind, earned reputations as places where well-behaved ladies—often actually wearing hats and white gloves—enjoyed dainty luncheons. Well-distanced socially and psychically from the bohemian dens of Greenwich Village, the Gypsy tea shops, and the artsy college-town hangouts, department store tea rooms established and maintained a standard of bourgeois decorum where good manners were required and ladyhood was cherished.

Wanamaker's in Philadelphia instituted the first department-store food service, in 1877. Like other department stores, it did not open a tea room until later. If an 1893 New York City guidebook is to be believed, the restaurants that stores operated before the tea room era were not always the finest eating places. "Several of the large bazaar stores, like Macy's and Hearn's, have restaurants [which] are not first-class in cooking or service," reported *King's Handbook of New York*. "It is the bargain counter extended to the lunch table, and you always feel that it is bargain-day comestibles that you are getting." Macy's had opened its ladies' lunchroom on the second floor in 1878. In 1904, Macy's introduced a Japanese tea room on the fifth floor of the new Herald Square store, adjoining the grocery department. In Chicago, Marshall Field opened its tea room in 1890, becoming the first department store to do so. The Denver Dry Goods Tearoom began around 1907, and year later a tea room was in operation in the L.S. McCabe & Co. store in Rock Island, Illinois. A few years after the new Wanamaker store opened in 1902, it advertised that its tea room served specially imported tea and "prides itself on its quaint service."

Not every department store contained a tea room or operated its own. A survey of department stores in 1933 found that only 44 percent of the sixty-two stores polled had tea rooms, and that some of these were fountain tea rooms limited to counter service. McCreery's and Lord & Taylor are the only department store tea rooms listed in a 1916 New York City guidebook. The 1933 study also revealed that while most of the stores ran their own tea rooms, a fifth of them were leased to outside op-

erators. At the Steiger's store in Springfield, Massachusetts, for instance, the Charles Hall Galleries, which sold fine china and table appointments, ran the Luncheon and Tea Balcony. In 1930, Mrs. A.W. Adams, who had been president of the Ohio Restaurant Association, partly owned the tea room at the Lindner Company Store on Euclid Avenue in Cleveland, which she had managed for fourteen years. Miss Vincent's Tea Room, presumably run by an actual Miss Vincent, was located in the William Hengerer Company Store in Buffalo, New York. New York's venerable Maillard's operated a tea room in Stern's in the 1920s.

Other types of stores also had tea rooms, some predating those in department stores. At Madame Demorest's Emporium of Fashion in New York City, for instance, women customers were served Mandarin tea in a room hung with Chinese silk panels while viewing gowns and paper dress patterns in the 1870s. Madame Ellen Demorest, an early believer in women's rights, was a backer of real estate tycoon Susan A. King's Asian-tea-importing company, whose distributors were women. Around 1910, the Yamato Bazaar in Los Angeles served free tea and cakes in its second-floor Japanese tea garden decorated with ferns, wisteria, wind chimes, and lanterns. In St. Louis, the Prufrock-Litton Furniture Company, whose new 1909 building occupied an entire city block at Fourth and St. Charles, operated a French tea garden in the store. In the 1920s the Brack Shops, selling home furnishings on West Seventh in Los Angeles, provided full dining-room service in its twelfth-floor Windsor Tea Rooms. On the top floor of Barker Brothers furniture store in Los Angeles was one of the city's revered Mary Louise tea rooms, a branch of Mary Louise's main location at 605 West Seventh. Wolferman's Tea Room in Kansas City, Missouri, was in the Wolferman's grocery store. Stehr's, an old mansion converted into women's specialty shops in Oshkosh, Wisconsin, had a tea room, which won a Duncan Hines seal of approval in 1937.

Beyond being an advertisement for the store, a tea room performed a number of other functions. Sometimes, given the amount of space a tea room occupied and its limited hours of operation, it was run at a loss simply to keep customers from leaving the store for lunch—with the risk that they might not return. Tea rooms did not always lose money, though. According to a 1930 survey, department store tea rooms had higher check averages than any type of eating places other than hotel and club dining rooms. Marshall Field in Chicago, Scruggs-Vandervoort-Barney in St. Louis, D.H. Holmes in New Orleans, and the George Innes Company in Wichita were prominent among those that made a profit from their tea rooms in the 1940s. A store's tea room showcased and promoted merchandise from other departments, especially through fashion shows held in the tea room or via adjoining gift shops and candy departments.

Because of the lower ratio of profit to floor space compared to other departments, tea rooms were usually located on a top floor, a poor retail location. If a tea room had a soda fountain, however, it was likely to be on a lower floor. The Meyer Brothers store in Paterson, New Jersey, for instance, put its tea room in a second-floor annex, along with its soda foun-

THE MEZZANINE TEA ROOM, THE GREEN JOYCE CO., STORE, COLUMBUS, OHIO.

MEZZANINE TEA ROOMS IN DEPARTMENT STORES TENDED TO BE INFORMAL AND OFTEN INCLUDED SODA FOUNTAINS.

tain and candy department. In Pittsburgh, the Frank & Seder store had a tea room and soda fountain on a lower-floor balcony.

Best Places to Eat

In many cities and towns, department store tea rooms were considered among the finest eating places. This was especially true in smaller cities, where the department store served as a bedrock institution in the heart of downtown. Meyer Brothers, occupying an entire city block, was virtually synonymous with Paterson. Meier & Frank's tea room in Portland, Oregon, was said to be one of the top dining spots in that city, if not the entire Pacific coast. In Washington, Rhodes Brothers' restful green sixth-floor tea room was Tacoma's best, while the Glass Block Store Tea Room in Duluth, Minnesota, billed itself as "the cosiest, daintiest place" in town in 1914.

In Kalamazoo, Michigan, anyone who showed up at Gilmore Brothers Tea Room on Burdick Street after noon was going to have a long wait in line. The James Black Dry Goods Company Tea Room, on East Fourth Street in Waterloo, Iowa, was known for its terrific 50¢ dinner in the early 1940s. The George Innes Company in Wichita devoted its entire upper floor to a tea room, with accompanying private dining rooms, and did a large dinner as well as luncheon business. In Sioux Falls, South Dakota, shoppers enjoyed lunch and tea in the Shriver-Johnson store, with dinner service on Monday nights.

Given their popularity and the large size of their dining rooms, the number of meals served in department store tea rooms could be enormous. One Saturday in the early 1920s the F. & R. Lazarus store in Columbus, Ohio, served 1,243 meals in its popular-priced balcony section alone. (Most meals were priced from 25¢ to 45¢ so that workingwomen could afford to eat there.) Wanamaker's could seat fourteen hundred people in its Grand Crystal Tea Room and served an average of 3,000 meals a day year-round. Before Christmas, shoppers thronged the tea rooms. On Thursday, December 7, 1922, Marshall Field served 8,642 meals.

Guidebooks invariably ranked department store tea rooms as good choices for travelers. Duncan Hines raved about Marshall Field and Carson Pirie Scott in Chicago, noting that the latter had a special elevator to its men's grill. He also recommended the tea room in the Harris Company store in San Bernardino, California, and the Daniels and Fisher tea room in Denver. In Connecticut, he applauded both Hartford's G. Fox tea room ("immaculate and delightful") and the Laurelette at Steiger's (where all the cooks were women). Along with the usual big-city favorites like Halle Brothers Tea Room in Cleveland, Carl Barrett's *Best Places to Eat* in 1942 singled out Herpolsheimer's Tea Room in Grand Rapids, Michigan, and O'Neil's Tea Room in Akron, Ohio. *Gourmet's Guide to Good*

Eating in 1948 mentioned the Wiley Department Store Tea Room in Hutchinson, Kansas, Dayton's Tiffin Room, and the Young Quinlan Tea Room in Minneapolis, Minnesota, as well as the Penthouse Tea Room at Neiman Marcus in Dallas.

Chicken Pies and Diet Plates

Because a store's reputation was linked to its tea room, the food served there had to be well prepared and of the highest quality. Professional home economists often managed and staffed department store tea rooms, making certain that the meals were nutritious and attractive. Plates were decorated with olives, lettuce, parsley, and pimiento at a time when these garnishes were mainly found in high-priced restaurants. Patrons expected food to be unusual and interesting, an expectation that applied to tea rooms generally. As a consequence, noted Mabel Little, dietitian and director of the tea room at LaSalle & Koch in Toledo, the manager had to be ever on the alert for "new dishes and combinations."

Vandervoort's tea room in St. Louis featured a new dish that caught the attention of a guest in 1920, consisting of a frozen cream-cheese fruit salad. On another downtown street in the same city, Stix Baer & Fuller complemented a seafood plate with toasted anchovy rolls. In Los Angeles, popular items on the tea room menu at Bullocks Wilshire store included stuffed zucchini, as well as orange, date-nut, and cheese breads. At Bullocks downtown, a 1930s menu featured a Spanish plate made up of small tamales, beans, salad, and toasted cheese sandwiches. Favorites at Filene's in Boston were chicken à la king, chop suey, and maple layer pie.

The Salad Bowl

Filene's Restaurant

PATRONS AT FILENE'S SALAD BOWL TEA ROOM COULD CHOOSE FROM CINNAMON TOAST (15¢), AFTERNOON TEA CAKES (15¢), OR A SLICED EGG, BEET, AND TOMATO SALAD (35¢), AMONG OTHER LIGHT DISHES ON THIS MENU.

Avoiding the obvious, Philadelphia's Strawbridge & Clothier replaced the standard chicken in their club sandwich with fried oysters, calling it a Rockaway Club Sandwich.

Every department store tea room had a specialty for which it was particularly known. Chicken pie served this role for many, including Marshall Field, Halle Brothers in Cleveland, J.L. Hudson in Detroit, Z.C.M.I. in Salt Lake City, and H.C. Capwell in Oakland (which also specialized in "frigid salad bowls"). At the Miller & Paine tea room in Lincoln, Nebraska, their chicken pies were memorable for having double crusts. Crispy-topped cinnamon rolls were another special feature. L.S. Ayres in Indianapolis was known for its chicken velvet soup as well as frozen pecan balls with fudge sauce. Customers at Burdine's in Miami appreciated their homemade pastries and rolls. Hutzler's Tea Room in Baltimore made crab dishes their specialty, while supplying hurried diners with salad trays in their sixth-floor Quixie. At O'Neil's in Akron, the favorites were corn sticks and homemade pies, and at Rich's in Atlanta they were tossed vegetable salad bowls and cream waffles.

Diet plates were popularized by department store tea rooms. In 1929, Toledo's LaSalle & Koch tea room offered the eighteen-day Mayo Clinic diet of grapefruit, tomatoes, eggs, and lettuce made famous by Ethel Barrymore. Bullock's Wilshire encouraged dieting in the 1930s with its "streamline luncheon," and its vegetable plate of grilled tomatoes, mushrooms, string beans, peas, asparagus, squash, and celery. The William H. Block store's Terrace Tea Room in Indianapolis had a 1944 menu with a "low-calory complete luncheon salad" of julienne chicken, ham, lettuce, egg, tomato, and spinach, accompanied by Ry-Krisps. This was during the war, so dieters were further aided by shortages of butter and cream, which restricted each diner to one serving. In Akron, O'Neil's Tea Room offered a porterhouse steak on its May 14, 1936, menu, under the heading "Diet Foods (That do not fatten)."

Teatime in department stores brought out another selection of delectable things to eat, plus a greater range of teas than found in most tea rooms. Delicate tea sandwiches were made of fig, lettuce, watercress, and combinations like cheese and bar-le-duc. A black-walnut relish sandwich costing 25¢ appeared on the afternoon tea menu at Lazarus in the early 1920s. At Filene's Salad Bowl, one could choose a baby chicken-salad sandwich and bread-and-butter sandwiches, plus a dessert from the 50¢ menu ("No gratuities permitted"). LaSalle & Koch's 1920 menu included a cheese dream for 30¢, and the tea room standby, a tomato stuffed with chicken salad, for an expensive 80¢. Under beverages, the menu had a pot of Ming Cha tea ("The Most Expensive Tea Grown") for 20¢. Around 1920, Mandel Brothers in Chicago gave tea drinkers a choice of oolong, English breakfast, uncolored Japan, Young Hyson, Ceylon, orange pekoe, and Gunpowder.

AFTERNOON TEA IN THE MARSHALL FIELD WALNUT ROOM IN 1909, THEN KNOWN AS THE SOUTH TEA ROOM. (*Chicago Daily News* photograph, Chicago Historical Society)

HOBBING WITH THE NOBS AT FIELD'S

Few department stores have had closer relationships with their city's elite than Marshall Field, a store designed so that its female customers never had to stoop to view merchandise. From the tea room's start in 1890 it served as a club for the wives and daughters of the rich and powerful. With only fifteen tables, and almost hidden in a corner of the fur department, it still managed to make an impression. On the day of its opening about sixty people ordered from hand-embroidered linen menus, which were to be laundered each day. Maids served orange punch, in orange shells garnished with smilax, and rose punch, ice cream with sauce served on a plate with a rose. Sandwiches arrived in baskets tied with ribbons.

The second year, Harriet Tilden (Harriet Vaughn Moody) was hired by manager Harry Gordon Selfridge, later the founder of Selfridge's in London, to supply gingerbread cakes and chicken salad, providing the basis for what would become her fashionable, upper-class catering business, the Home Delicacies Association. At first she baked the cakes twenty-four at a time in her home oven. Other women prepared codfish cakes and Boston baked beans, delivering them to the store each morning. Field's menus stuck to the tried-and-true, with the corned beef hash that appeared on the opening day menu becoming one of its patrons' all-time favorites.

The initial tea room proved so popular it had to be expanded. It moved several times, each time growing larger. In 1902 it went to the seventh floor, and a men's grill room was opened. Additional rooms were added, until the tea rooms totaled seven in the early 1920s and served about five thousand meals a day. Along with a notice telling customers that a free page service was available, menus at that time announced, "The Tea Rooms of Marshall Field & Company reflect the character of an organization devoted to careful consideration of others."

A visitor in 1920 was delighted with bouillabaisse served in a little copper cauldron. At tea in the Narcissus Fountain room she was served triangular pieces of cinnamon toast, and an assortment of bread rounds spread with cream cheese, variously combined with pepper, chopped nuts, pineapple, and pimiento. A huge 1922 tea menu listed fourteen kinds of tea sandwiches, eleven kinds of pickles, thirty-seven salads, and seventy-two ready-to-serve hot dishes. Orange punch still appeared on the menu, but rose punch was gone. Potato-flour muffins, a wartime substitution that had become a hit, remained.

The tea rooms, which weathered the ups and downs of business cycles, continued to attract elites. In 1931, a Chicago guidebook observed of the Colonial Room, by then the only of the store's tea rooms in which smoking was forbidden, "The atmosphere is conservative and many feminine members of the pioneer first families of the city [come here for tea]."

Children, shoppers of the future, were always welcome in department store tea rooms. Menus designed for them with clowns, circuses, and zoo animals featured peanut butter sandwiches, vegetable plates, and lunches with fanciful names such as Little Red Hens (creamed chicken in a nest of whipped potatoes), Bull in the Pen (hamburger and fries), as well as Lambi-Pies and Jumbo the Elephants. At Carson Pirie Scott in Chicago, Saturday meant special Hobby Horse Luncheons for children. Woodward & Lothrop at 921 Pennsylvania in Washington, D.C., had a children's tea room with little tables and chairs. At the Hess store in Allentown, Pennsylvania, children's food arrived on tiny tin stoves.

Special Attractions

Sedate though they were, department store tea rooms had a lot to offer customers beyond good food at reasonable prices, such as attractive surroundings and a range of special events and services.

Men were appreciative of grill rooms reserved for their use. Menus in grill rooms and tea rooms were basically the same, but the word grill, the absence of women, and men's club-style furnishings signified to guests that they had entered a masculine sanctum sanctorum. The general rule was that men could eat in the tea room but women could not eat in the grill room. (A few exceptions were made: at Carson Pirie Scott women were welcome on Saturdays—but only if escorted by a man.) Filene's had no grill room, but cordoned off a portion of its eighth-floor tea room for men, permitting them to smoke. Tacoma's Rhodes Brothers tea room had no grill in 1910 but assured men "you won't feel out of place at all."

Wanamaker's, on the other hand, had an entire "men's section" consisting of three rooms to the east of the Grand Crystal Tea Room. At Wanamaker's and elsewhere it is likely that men were the principal users of many of the smaller meeting rooms. Fourteen civic clubs met in Rich's tea rooms in Atlanta in the early 1940s.

Grill room decor was similar to that found in many of the better restaurants and hotel dining rooms of the early 1920s. Carson's grill seated seven hundred and was furnished in Elizabethan oak paneling, with a black tile floor, and dark oak chairs with red leather upholstery. At Mandel's, also in Chicago, a pictorial frieze ran above the oak wainscoting, ceilings were beamed, and the floor was red and black tile. Leaded-glass windows, velvet draperies, and low lights contributed to the feeling of being in a baronial castle. The grill at F. & R. Lazarus in Columbus, Ohio, also had oak paneling, as did the Spokane Dry Goods Company. Plush booths with large round tables along grill room walls often attracted small groups of men who would gather at "their" table each day.

Tea rooms also furnished entertainment to their guests, in the form of fashion shows, music, dancing, bridge, and mah-jongg. A spectacular fashion show with a Monte Carlo theme at Gimbel's in Manhattan drew thousands of spectators in 1911. In rooms decorated with roulette tables and Mediterranean gardens, models showed off the latest Paris fashions, walking on a promenade that stretched from the theater to the tea room. Many tea rooms, among them Bullock's Wilshire, Rich's in Atlanta, and Younkers in Des Moines had weekly fashion shows at noon. Music entertained patrons of Columbus's Lazarus from eleven-thirty to two each day in the early 1920s. At Younkers, Philbrick and his Younkers Tea Room Orchestra entertained in the 1920s, while Barney Barnard played for dinner dancing on Saturdays in the 1940s. In the 1920s Filene's featured dancing every afternoon. Bridge and mah-jongg both gained great popularity in the 1920s, and many tea rooms catered to players. Each afternoon from two-thirty to five around 1922, Gimbel's offered "expert instruction" in mah-jongg for 75¢.

Younkers
Beautiful
Tea Room

Luncheon, 11:30 to 2:30
Tea, 2:30 to 5 p.m.
Dinner, 5:15 to 8 p.m.

DURING THE SECOND WORLD WAR, YOUNKERS TEA ROOM FEATURED $1.10 THEATER DINNERS AT WHICH EACH PATRON RECEIVED A FREE TICKET TO THE DES MOINES, PARAMOUNT, OR ROOSEVELT THEATERS.

Less exerting pastimes included celebrity-spotting in Bullock's Wilshire Desert Tea Room, where Gloria Swanson and other film stars were often seen in the 1930s. In other stores customers could simply enjoy the room's ambience or look out the window at the city below. Bullock's offered a nice view of palm-lined streets and the Hollywood hills, while patrons at Wanamaker's could see the Delaware River stretching from the Pennsylvania Railroad bridge to the League Island Navy Yard. A rare view of Peoria, Illinois, was possible from the seventh-floor tea room of Block & Kuhl. Guests at Capwell's wicker-furnished tea room in Oakland could stroll though French doors onto a Venetian roof garden complete with a shady pergola.

Some interiors also warranted closer examination. Although many department store tea rooms were located in huge banquet-style rooms with subdued decor, others were more interesting. The Wolff & Marx tea room in San Antonio, Texas, began as a plain lunchroom in 1913 but was transformed in the 1920s when the owners moved it to the top floor and spent a fortune creating a Japanese garden. Patrons entering the tea room crossed a stone bridge over a rock-lined stream stocked with goldfish. Bullock's Wilshire, a temple of art deco opened in 1929, decorated its Desert Tea Room with a cactus motif and a color scheme of soft pink and green. Even the Venetian blinds picked up the room's colors, with slats in alternating pink, green, and ivory. Around 1948 Lord & Taylor's Westchester Tea Room was done in postwar amoebic modern. A tree trunk penetrated the streamline ceiling, free-form partitions on poles divided up the space, and patrons sat in moderne upholstered chairs equipped with built-in trays.

Mind Your Manners

Something about department stores elevated them above purely commercial enterprises, affecting all departments within, including tea rooms. It was as though their founders had embarked on a civilizing mission or had taken an oath on a stack of *Ladies' Home Journals* to uphold the loftiest of middle-class standards. Wanamaker's epitomized this attitude. The original nineteenth-century store contained a tablet with an inscription by founder John Wanamaker that said, "Let those who follow me continue to build with the plumb of honor, the level of truth, and the square of integrity, education, courtesy, and mutuality." Whether it was because of so many department stores' formal beaux arts architecture, or the high ceilings within, customers tended to dress well and be on their best behavior while inside the store.

In many cases customers truly took a store's mission to heart. In cities with several department stores, families were likely to choose one and remain faithful to it for generations—just as they might do with their church. Those with an account at a store had only to sign their name on a tea room check to have the meal billed to them (real ladies didn't handle money). The close relationship between a store and its customers entailed risk. Stores knew that their customers were sensitive to anything they regarded as a breach of trust. It took years after Prohibition ended, for instance, before department stores could advertise cocktail glasses without hearing from outraged teetotaling customers who demanded to cancel their accounts.

The upright approach affected every detail of how tea rooms were conducted, from their appearance, policies, and food right down to the rules waitresses had to follow. The management of many department store tea rooms was entrusted to women trained in the profession of home economics. They too had a mission: to see that public kitchens were run hygienically and that they produced nutritious food of the highest quality. The kitchens at Marshall Field were said to be "exquisitely clean." In the 1930s all three Bullock's tea rooms in Los Angeles were managed by a Miss Larson, a paragon of her kind. "Everything she serves looks like a page from *Good Housekeeping* in its perfection," said a reviewer, "and tastes like the prize recipes of the greatest experts in domestic science."

Department store food service offered trained women one of the

best-paid positions in their field, and one of the few opportunities out-side an institutional setting. Helen Sawyer of Lazarus graduated from the University of Nebraska; all her assistants were also college women. Around 1930 she moved on to Younker Brothers, and in 1933 she was elected to a directorship of the National Restaurant Association, a rare po-sition for a woman then. Mildred Bettel Johnson, a Simmons graduate, managed the Halle Brothers tea room before she went to Joseph Horne in Pittsburgh, where in 1929 she oversaw all the store's food departments: a tea room, two cafeterias, a retail food counter, and a candy department. When Mrs. E.M. Evans took over the management of Pelletier's Tea Room in Topeka, Kansas, in 1925, the store printed a leaflet introducing her. She had been trained in tea room work at the Kansas State Agricultural Col-lege, it said, as well as the State University of California. "Luncheon and Dinner Parties under her guidance are a joy and pleasure. Her menus are delightfully new and daintily served," continued the leaflet, urging pa-trons to let her plan their parties.

The dietitian's hand could be seen in several menus of the early

1920s. The Lazarus menu had a section of "hygienic foods," which included shredded-wheat biscuits or toasted corn flakes with cream, bran muffins, and cream toast. If those choices sounded too complex, the diner could opt for a "bowl of cream with bread or crackers." Filene's chemically tested all the food it served for purity and included "Fleischmann's Yeast, with toasted crackers for your health" for 10¢ on its tea menu. A good range of vegetables appeared on menus too. Beyond the usual peas and carrots, choices might include Brussels sprouts in cream, buttered turnips, sautéed eggplant, California asparagus, sugar beets, and creamed cauliflower.

Tea room employees—almost exclusively women—were expected to adhere to a long list of rules, which often included not accepting tips. "Tips do not form a part of our service," announced the Lazarus menu. An early 1920s Filene's manual said, "Accepting tips of any kind will mean immediate discharge. If money is left on the table, it must be reported to the head waitress, who will collect it and turn it over to [a fund]." Filene's rules also forbade waitresses to wear fancy combs, jewelry, or tortoiseshell glasses and instructed them to wear a white skirt under their uniform. Lest the manual seem too negative, it furnished an inspirational message: "We want you to accept a new thought. That you are not waitresses alone—but Hostesses—receiving all day the Guests of this House."

Department stores made sure their guests—who were likely to view all waitresses with prejudice—would consider their staff members "respectable." All the waitresses in the Daniel and Fisher Tower Tea Room in 1928 were over forty years old. At Marshall Field, applicants were asked for character references and carefully screened, a generally uncommon practice in the restaurant trade. According to a 1920 account, waitresses there reacted to strict rules with a mild form of rebellion. During breaks they amused themselves by mocking their supervisor. "I hear you've taken to drink, Fannie," a waitress jokingly said to a fellow worker who had violated the rules by sipping from a glass of water on the serving floor. Another then said, "You may do that elsewhere but not at [Marshall Field's]." And a third said solemnly, "Do you not realize, Fannie, that you are part of a great organization?"

A sense of decorum was imparted to tea room patrons by the formality of the large rooms, which often had high ceilings, massive columns, crystal chandeliers, floral arrangements, and fine table appointments. Some tea rooms even had finger bowls and silver sugar tongs. As a suitably impressed diner at Younker's succinctly wrote, "Quiet, dignified appearance lends place an air." According to Wanamaker's 1926 booklet, the Grand Crystal Tea Room was "in the mode of the Renaissance." San Francisco's White House tea room, operated by Raphael Weill, was decorated in the grand European dining-room tradition, with elaborate Versailles-like plasterwork, high windows with shirred-silk draperies, and floor-to-ceiling mirrors. If the rooms themselves were not sufficiently intimidating, ladylike behavior was further encouraged by prohibitions against women smoking (though men were permitted to smoke in the grill rooms). Department store tea rooms proved themselves valuable training grounds for good manners and were often used by mothers determined to instill ladylike behavior in recalcitrant daughters.

❖ ❖ ❖

Suburbanization, national chain ownership, and a faster pace of life would eventually undermine department store tea rooms. Management shut down central-city stores entirely or closed their "old-fashioned" tea rooms. If a branch store had a tea room, it tended to be smaller since less floor space was devoted to food service. Now forced to be a "money-maker," its furnishings would be casual and not conducive to leisurely dining. As one department store executive put it in 1949, "There is a subtle relationship, in any food operation, between profit and uncomfortable chairs. Put a customer on a stool and he will eat his sandwich and get out to make room for another customer; but give him nice surroundings and an easy chair and he will dawdle the afternoon away." To further streamline operations, department stores whittled down their menus, eliminating afternoon tea and featuring quick lunch specials more in keeping with luncheonettes than stately dining rooms. Little by little, the grande dame department store tea room all but vanished.

CHAPTER EIGHT

Conclusion

Ladies Tearooms Are a Dying Breed.

—*NEW YORK TIMES* HEADLINE, AUGUST 3, 1973

Reports of my death are greatly exaggerated.

—MARK TWAIN

The long-term effects of the tea room craze are still felt today, in ways few people suspect. Tea rooms introduced candles and flowers to restaurant tables. They brought homestyle food, domestic decorating schemes, and a less grandiose sense of style into public dining rooms. They made dining outdoors popular. They proved that people eating away from home would order humble dishes like egg salad and bread pudding, especially if they were prepared well and served attractively. Tea rooms restyled restaurant interiors, cultivating atmosphere. They replaced Oriental carpets with rag rugs, chandeliers with intimate shaded lamps, and damask draperies with homespun curtains. They popularized bare tabletops with informal place mats and paper napkins instead of table linens. Inspired by Colonial tavern signs, they introduced a whole new kind of (literally) colorful restaurant names in place of formerly dominant family surnames. They hired college girls as waitresses and substituted friendly hostesses for stiffly tuxedoed maître d's. They demonstrated that women could succeed in the restaurant industry and that money could be made in the food business even without alcohol. They showed that women were a solid customer base and that families with children could be accommodated. Greenwich Village tea rooms, in particular, foreshadowed the beatnik coffeehouse movement of the 1950s and 1960s, which in turn inspired the independent coffee bars of today.

Tea rooms have made a comeback in recent years. Ironically, and maybe because of the depletion of Colonial themes and unfamiliarity with the Greenwich Village era, many of them have been interpreted as "Victorian," thus obscuring the mostly twentieth-century history of this fascinating and culturally fertile institution. But, looked at differently, it may be that the Victorian age symbolizes for women of the early twenty-first century something very similar to what the Colonial period meant to their early twentieth-century ancestors. For both, the past may represent a warmer, sweeter, more hospitable time. All in all, throughout a century in which they have waxed and waned and waxed again, appearing in a variety of forms and guises, tea rooms have proved to be an enduring and well-loved institution of women's culture.

SELECTED BIBLIOGRAPHY

This book was researched using a vast number of sources, some containing only small bits of information. Menus, brochures, postcards, guidebooks, city directories, vintage women's magazines, and archival collections all contributed mightily. The following list is a sampling of sources and contains books primarily. Some of the books are in print, but many can only be found in libraries and antiquarian-bookstores—if the searcher is both persistent and lucky. Women's magazines from the late 1910s and the 1920s contain a wealth of information on tea rooms, and several of the more inclusive articles are listed here.

Beard, Rick, and Leslie Cohen Berlowitz, eds., 1993. *Greenwich Village: Culture and Counterculture*. New Brunswick, N.J.: Rutgers University Press.

Belasco, Warren James, 1979. *Americans on the Road: From Autocamp to Motel, 1910–1945*. Cambridge: MIT Press.

Bradley, Alice, 1922. *Cooking for Profit*. Chicago: American School of Home Economics.

Brandimarte, Cynthia, 1995. "To Make the Whole World Homelike: Gender, Space, and America's Tea Room Movement." *Winterthur Portfolio* 30, no. 1.

Chapin, Anna Alice, 1917. *Greenwich Village*. New York: Dodd, Mead & Co.

Chappell, George S., 1925. *The Restaurants of New York*. New York: Greenberg Publisher, Inc.

Claudy, C.H., 1916. "Organizing the Wayside Tea House." *Country Life in America*, June.

Dahl, Joseph Oliver, 1927. *Restaurant Management*. New York: Harper and Bros. Publishers.

Donovan, Frances, 1920. *The Woman Who Waits*. Boston: Richard G. Badger. Reprinted by Arno Press, 1974.

Drury, John, 1931. *Dining in Chicago*. New York: The John Day Co.

Dudley, Herminie, and Sarah Leyburn Coe, 1911. "Taverns and Tea Rooms as a Business for Women." *Good Housekeeping*, June.

Elliott, Ralph Nelson, 1926. *Tea Room and Cafeteria Management*. Boston: Little, Brown & Co.

Fales, Winnifred, and Mary Northend, 1917. "At the Sign of the Tea-Room." *Good Housekeeping*, July.

SELECTED BIBLIOGRAPHY

Fowler, Grace A., 1908. "The Development of the Tea-room." *Harper's Bazar*, March.

Hines, Duncan, 1936. *Adventures in Good Eating for the Discriminating Motorist*. Bowling Green, Ky.: Self-published.

Jordan, Charlotte B., 1911. "The Tea-Room by the Wayside." *Ladies' Home Journal*, May 15.

Levenstein, Harvey, 1988. *Revolution at the Table: The Transformation of the American Diet*. New York: Oxford University Press.

MacDougall, Alice Foote, 1926. *Coffee and Waffles*. Garden City and New York: Double-day, Page & Company.

————, 1928. *The Autobiography of a Business Woman*. Boston: Little, Brown, and Co.

————, 1929. *The Secret of Successful Restaurants*. New York: Harper & Bros.

Nichols, May Ellis, 1925. "Naming the Tea-Room." *American Cookery*, December.

Overbaugh, Kathryn, 1937. "Tea Room Rejuvenation." *American Cookery*, October.

Ware, Caroline F., 1935. *Greenwich Village, 1920–30*. Boston: Houghton-Mifflin Co. Reprinted by the University of California Press, 1994.

Woman's Institute of Domestic Arts & Sciences, Inc., 1932. *The Tea Room and Coffee Shop*. Scranton, Pa.: International Textbook Co.

Zorbaugh, Harvey Warren, 1929. *The Gold Coast and the Slum*. Chicago: University of Chicago Press.

Note: Illustrations are indicated in **bold**